BETRAYAL

BETRAYAL

France, the Arabs, and the Jews

BY

DAVID PRYCE-JONES

ENCOUNTER BOOKS
NEW YORK

First edition published in 2006 by Encounter Books, an activity of Encounter for Culture and Education, Inc., a nonprofit, tax exempt corporation. Encounter Books website address: *www.encounterbooks.com*

Manufactured in the United States and printed on acid-free paper. The paper used in this publication meets the minimum requirements of ANSI/NISO Z39.48-1992 (R 1997)(*Permanence of Paper*).

FIRST EDITION

LIBRARY OF CONGRESS CATALOGING-IN-PUBLICATION DATA
Pryce-Jones, David
Betrayal: France, the Arabs, and the Jews/David Pryce-Jones
p.   cm.
ISBN 1-59403-151-7
1. France—Foreign relations—middle east. 2.Middle East—Foreign relations—France. 3. France—Foreign relations—Israel. 4. Israel—Foreign relations—France. 5. France—Foreign relations—1945. 6. Middle East—Politics and government—20th century. 7. Middle East-History—20th century. 8. Arabs—France—Political activity.
I. title.
DC59.8.L4P79 2006
327.44056—dc22
2006022185

10 9 8 7 6 5 4 3 2 1

For Neal Kozodoy

CONTENTS

THE TEST FOR much of the world today comes from political Islam. The phenomenon is complex, to be sure, to do with self-perception on the part of Muslims and non-Muslims, the end of empire, globalization, and much else besides. Dramatic events such as 9/11, the campaigns in Afghanistan and Iraq, and Iran's nuclear ambitions are in the process of evolving a balance of power between political Islam and the West that will determine the future for a long time ahead.

I have long been struck by the way that French rulers and intellectuals have habitually described France as a Muslim power. By this unlikely expression, they meant that France was well placed to take advantage of Muslims either under direct rule in what were once colonies and protectorates, or otherwise within the French sphere of influence in more recent years when Muslim countries had gained independence. It did not occur to those who thought like this that one day the position might be reversed, and Muslims could take advantage of a France within an Islamic sphere of influence.

As a small child, in a family with French relations,

Preface

I found myself in France in the terrible year of 1940. The famous Maginot line, it had been generally assumed, would keep the country safe as a great and independent power. Among France's proudest contributions to democracy and civilization are authorship and pursuit of the Rights of Man, and nationalism, the sense of nationhood that has a direct and intimate relationship to rights. When the test with Nazism came to a head, nationalism failed, the nation collapsed, and mass-murder replaced the Rights of Man. The armed intervention of its Allies alone saved France from a fate as a vassal in an alien empire.

French foreign policy is the preserve of the Quai d'Orsay, the ministry in charge of its administration, and its archives provide evidence down the generations to the present of the translation into practice of the concept of France as a Muslim power. As a result of policies stemming from this way of looking at things, disastrous consequences have long been accumulating at home as in the Middle East. Intellectually, this approach to the Arab and Muslim world has been what the Maginot Line was militarily, a masking of reality, a standing invitation to self-deception.

Closely following the ministry's own documentation and the testimony of its officials, *Betrayal: France, the Arabs, and the Jews* chronicles how in pursuit of what it has deemed to be a prime national interest France has only done injury to itself and raised the level of instability and violence in the world. The record shows that its policies towards Arabs and Jews have been consistently misguided as well as untrue to the values France once claimed to exemplify in the name of enlightenment. Those in charge of French foreign policy in these areas have simultaneously betrayed the national inerest and democracy itself. This is the context in which the country and the continent of Europe, not to say the West, now has to confront the test of political Islam.

BETRAYAL

ONE

The Harvest

CLICHY-SOUS-BOIS, nine miles north-east of Paris, is a suburb in the brutalist style, all concrete, high rises, and right angles. In this inauspicious setting, violence flared up on October 27, 2005, leapfrogging immediately to other identical municipalities of the capital and so on to some three hundred cities and towns right across France. Night after night, rioters set fire to cars; they hurled petrol bombs and battled with the police and firemen. Copy-cats, the rioters appeared to have no program, no demands except to enjoy license to behave as they pleased. Theirs was a very modern insurgency, a simple rage against the way things are.

Caught by surprise, the authorities hardly knew how to react, but after a while they imposed curfews and declared a state of emergency. By the following January, the violence, though still routine all over the country, had ebbed to levels low enough for the authorities to turn a blind eye and pretend that calm and normality was once more the order of the day. Prime Minister Dominique de Villepin then informed deputies in the National Assembly that 8,500 vehicles of all sorts had just been burnt, over a hundred public buildings and as many private businesses or offices had been damaged or destroyed, 125 policemen were wounded, and 600 of the 2,800 rioters arrested were behind bars. By March 2006, revised figures stated that around 10,000 vehicles been burnt, 230 buildings damaged or destroyed, and 800 of the 5,000 arrested had received prison sentences. The annual toll was far higher. According to official statistics, in the course of 2005 there were 110,206 recorded incidents of urban violence, and 45,588 vehicles had been burnt out. For a leading commentator like Nicolas Baverez, the enormity of it illustrates "national crisis and the decomposition of the social body."

Neither Villepin nor anyone else liked to concentrate on the human horrors of the moment: a man lynched for taking an art photograph of a lamp-post; a resident of Stains beaten to death for trying to stop a fire; a handicapped woman on a bus soaked in petrol and set on fire; a journalist from Korea beaten unconscious; and above all two teenagers, the one Moroccan and the other from Mauritania, whose deaths had triggered this whole sequence of events. In Clichy-sous-Bois where they lived, these two jumped over a fence into an electricity substation and were electrocuted. Either they were being pursued by the police for some reason, or imagined they were—it is not clear which.

Interpreting the insurgency, officialdom and opinion-

4

makers alike sank into the comfortable shallows of sociology, where simple rage could be rationalized into something else. The two electrocuted teenagers—and the rioters who threw Molotov cocktails (and the few who fired shots) supposedly to avenge them—were defined as victims, not delinquents. Poor housing, ghetto neighborhoods, unemployment, a sense of alienation, had to be the causes of the violence. Giving an unmistakable clue to their motivation, rioters themselves had shouted "Allahu akhbar" as they burnt cars, but the obvious conclusion might sound provocative, and so they were categorized as immigrants, North Africans and blacks, nihilists, vandals, anything but the Arabs and Muslims they actually were. Other immigrant minorities, for instance the Vietnamese or Chinese, had not rioted, but even so it was conveniently agreed that what had just happened could not be called an intifada, and even less jihad. In an interview with an Israeli newspaper (afterwards translated into French), the well-known liberal philosopher Alain Finkielkraut rather timidly advanced the proposition that the rioting might be racist on the part of the Arabs and Muslims. Vilified by everyone who was anyone, more or less ostracized, he was speedily obliged to retract. On the radio, Philippe de Villiers, a conservative politician, was one of the very few to speak of the "Islamization" of minds and territory and even free speech.

Some on the Left and in the media went so far as to affirm that the French should apologize for bringing this insurgency upon themselves. Fastening the word "scum" (*racaille*) on to those responsible for urban lawlessness on this scale, and proposing in a half-meant jest to turn high-powered water-hoses on them, Nicolas Sarkozy, the Minister of the Interior, was widely held to have been guilty of bad judgment and needless provocation. Other ministers before him had accepted for the sake of live-and-let-live that Arabs and Muslims could carve out un-policed or no-go areas for themselves, obedient, as it were, only to their own exclusive law, a far-out version of the sharia, the law of Muslims. And some of the blame could also be ascribed to sheer bad luck. In the face of a mob at one point, the police were resorting to tear gas, and a canister had landed in a large and crowded mosque during prayers. This was an accident, the police were quick to assure everybody, while in the same breath apologizing for the way it had inflamed Muslim opinion.

France has long taken pride in its resounding slogan of "liberty, equality, fraternity," and these values leave no room for racism, at least in theory. All have only to subscribe to the republican social compact on the Republic's own terms. Immigrants, refugees, and exiles had long been arriving from everywhere round the globe and settling in France. An old-style music-hall song once celebrated their hugely varied backgrounds with the cheerful refrain, *"et tout ça, ça fait d'excellents Français"* (and all that [i.e., the many peoples listed in the lyrics] makes for excellent Frenchmen). In practice, however, over the two centuries since the revolution, rulers of France have tried to fit two peoples with particular views of themselves—Arabs and Jews—into their grand design for the nation and its standing in the world. Today, as a result of these

6

long-held but misconceived ambitions, racism with its hates and fears increasingly plagues France, calling into question the relationship that the country's Arab and Jewish minorities have with one another, that each have with the state, and that the state has with Arab nations on the one hand and with Israel on the other.

Although virtually no Muslims lived in France until the twentieth century, the French state traditionally regarded its interests as tied up in Arab and Muslim lands. Napoleon Bonaparte's 1798 campaign in Egypt and the French invasion of Algeria in 1830 were military adventures undertaken with the express purpose of emulating imperial Britain. The British might have India, but the French could move into, and ultimately colonize, the Arab world. Moreover, France claimed the right to protect Catholics and Christianity in the Ottoman Empire, and by that means legitimize a presence in the Holy Land. In response to a similar British appointment, Comte Gabriel de Lantivy in 1843 opened the French consulate in Jerusalem. He had served as an officer under Bonaparte. In his first despatch to Paris, Lantivy confirmed that the government had sent him to the Holy Land "to defend the Rights and the interests of Christians." In the 1850s, Napoleon III and his administration further elaborated for the first time the concept of a "Franco-Arab kingdom," grandiosely expanding this to visualize for the first time the concept of France itself as a Muslim power (*"une puissance musulmane"*). Designed to justify colonialism, here was a fantasy with no basis in reality but nevertheless captivating and heady enough to survive unscathed from the Second Empire to the Fifth Republic.

North African Arabs fought in large numbers in the French army in the First War and in colonial campaigns, sometimes against fellow Muslims. To reward them for their loyal service, the Great Mosque of Paris was opened in 1926. Large-scale Arab immigration did not begin until after the Evian Agreement ending the Algerian war in 1962, when almost one hundred thousand so-called "*harkis*," or Algerians who had opposed the nationalist movement, sought shelter and safety in France (and as many again who stayed in their native country were massacred by the victorious nationalists). Nobody at the time predicted that this might mark the beginning of a population movement with the potential of radically changing the social composition of France, or that "With the Algerian war, colonial racism starts its crossing of the Mediterranean," in the striking words of Benjamin Stora, a historian of Algeria. In the 1960s and 1970s, immigrants arrived steadily from each of the newly independent Maghreb countries. Initially they were allowed to come only as guest workers seeking to better themselves and then return home, but a change of law in 1974 gave them residence and other rights.

The size of today's community is a matter of contention. The law forbids census-takers from asking the religion of respondents. A figure of upward of six million has long been accepted, though some scare-mongering estimates are still higher. Nicolas Sarkozy and the semiofficial newspaper *Le Monde* have both used the figure of five million. Michèle Tribalat, a demographer, has reduced this further to 3.65 million. Demographic extrapolations are notoriously untrustworthy, but some profess to show that in fifteen or so years as much as a quarter of the French population may be Muslim and Arab, comprising, that is to say, a minority different from the majority in respects both religious and cultural, and large enough to reject integration—should it so choose—on the terms advanced by the majority.

The recent insurgency revealed the extent to which Muslims and Arabs congregate in the banlieues or out-skirts of the great cities, and where they are now in the process of determining whether they will indeed inte-grate or alternatively choose separatism—in other words whether their identity is to be primarily French, or French-Muslim, or plain Muslim. The number of mosques is usually given as around 1,600 but some more informal places of worship and prayer rooms seem not to be accounted for. Mosques serve as community centers and there appear to be 1,500 imams in the country. Some among them speak no French and a few reject integration with a fury for which reverse colonial-ism is the only apposite term. An example of a wholly politicized imam is Chelali Benchallali, who has been preaching jihad in Vénissieux, a suburb of Lyons. The imam's son and two others from Vénissieux were among the seven French prisoners held in Guantanamo. In his apartment, the imam himself had a chemical lab-oratory manufacturing ricin bombs.

At the national level there are representative Muslim institutions such as the French Council for the Muslim

Religion, or c f c m in its French acronym, and the Union
of Islamic Organizations in France, u o i f in its French
acronym. Tension exists between these two bodies, as the
former aspires to belong to the French establishment
while the latter is an off-shoot of the world-wide Muslim
Brotherhood, and as such stands for outright and sepa-
ratist political Islam. Some of the demands or practices of
Islam being incompatible with bedrock republican sec-
ularism, embarrassing conflicts have arisen like the one
over the right of Muslim girls to wear the hijab in schools.
The authorities hesitated for fifteen years before deciding
that this practice was unconstitutional. The after-shocks
of the recent violence serve to confirm that Muslims and
Arabs constitute an organized presence of such weight
and numbers that for electoral reasons alone no politician can afford to disregard it.

The official position taken towards French Jews dates
back to the revolution. In December 1789, the Comte de
Clermont-Tonnerre, a liberal aristocrat, declared in the
Constituent Assembly, "Everything must be refused to
the Jews as a nation and everything granted to the Jews
as individuals." This idea was soon enshrined in law.
Driving it was the suspicion that Jews indeed had their
own brand of nationalism, one that cut across the French
nationalism emerging with fervor from the revolution. To
the French elite, furthermore, this definition of Jews has
been a necessary and long-standing summons to loyalty
because Jews seemed to them all too often to be the conspiratorial tools of others, first of Germany and Russia,

then of Britain, finally of Zionists whose core doctrine is that Jews are a nation after all.

It is remarkable that in spite of the unregenerate anti-Semitism revealed and unleashed by the Dreyfus Affair at the end of the nineteenth century, and in spite even of French participation in the Nazi mass-murder of the last war, French Jews have generally accommodated to the state's view of the necessary relation between them, and have been content, at least until recently, to down-play the ethnic element in their own identity as a people. This has been less true of those who fled from the de-colonizing Arab states of North Africa, and who today make up the majority of the community, whose overall strength is estimated somewhere between five and six hundred thousand. In addition, the number of racist attacks against Jews or Jewish institutions rose from 69 in 1999 to as high as 932 in 2002 (though declining to 588 in 2003), and this has raised the ethnic conscious-ness of even the most assimilated elements of the older community. What happens in the Middle East has imme-diate repercussions on them. When the Israeli army moved in April 2002 against Palestinian terrorists in the West Bank town of Jenin, for instance, the Ministry of the Interior reported 395 anti-Jewish incidents around France (and *The New York Times* picked this up in an article on February 29, 2004).

Depending on the figures one accepts, Muslims and Arabs outnumber Jews in France by a factor of at least six to one, perhaps by as much as eight to one. As the number of Muslims and Arabs rises, and as France fails to deliver on its contemporary promise of fraternity, equality, and prosperity, the question of the relative place of these two minorities has come increasingly to the fore. The twentieth-century process of decolonization has made that question all the more complicated because Arabs and Jews alike have transformed themselves from passive subjects into active agents on the world's stage, acquiring new identities and in the end modern nation-states of their own.

For Arabs, one of the most evident tests of identity is hostility towards Jews and Israel. Traditional stereotypes and contemporary political preoccupations reinforce one another. Of course, Arab aggression against Jews has been rising everywhere in the last decades. But it is particularly virulent in France, and heightened because the authorities— virtually in denial—have pretended that the bombing of synagogues, restaurants, offices, and shops, and even the occasional loss of life, was mundane criminality rather than the manifestation of a jihad increasingly gathering strength. Agents of law enforcement are willing and able to crack down on terrorists, real or suspected, but reluctant to act against imams exploiting their mosques to glorify separatism and to instill anti-Semitism and hatred of non-believers in the minds of Muslims.

In an essay in *L'Islam en France*, a collection published in 2003 by Cités, Barbara Lefebvre offered typical examples of the skein of prejudice accumulating in the younger generation. Addressing the teacher, a boy in the Paris suburb of Saint-Denis quotes his father: "There will be a final war between Muslims and Jews, and the Jews will be destroyed; it says so in the Qur'an." In another Paris district, a teacher overhears Arab children telling Jewish children, "Jewish dog, we're going to burn Israel, go back to your country."

Olivier Guitta, a well-informed reporter, has recorded some of this Muslim anti-Semitism. He has described how in yet another school two Arab pupils were expelled for shouting "Dirty Jew" at a class-mate and beating him up. When the Arab aggressors filed a lawsuit against the school, the Paris tribunal ordered it to reinstate them and pay each of their families a thousand euros (around $1,200). In yet another incident, the police arrested Muslim teenagers who were beating up a young Jew at a skating rink in the Paris suburb of Boulogne. Releasing this group, the judge merely ordered one of them to write an essay on anti-Semitism. The group next attacked the son of the Boulogne rabbi and the same judge again released them unpunished. Shouting "Allahu akhbar," a Muslim stabbed Israel Ifrah, a Jewish student, and two other Muslims then spat at the family of the wounded man when they were waiting in the hospital.

In November 2003, Adel Boumedienne, of Algerian origins, cornered his neighbor, Sébastien Selam, a Jewish disc jockey, in the underground garage of the building where they both lived. He slit his victim's throat, almost decapitating him, and then gouged his eyes out with a carving fork. Coming upstairs with bloodied hands, he told his mother, "I killed my Jew, I will go to paradise."

Betrayal

In the spring of 2004, Madame Chirac, the President's wife, attended a gala concert at which one of the singers was Shirel, who is Jewish. Young Muslims in the front rows of the audience interrupted her performance yelling, "Dirty Jew. Death to the Jews. We'll kill you." As Guitta comments, "The loud silence of Mrs. Chirac speaks volumes."

Ilan Halimi was a twenty three year old shop assistant selling cell-phones and living in Bagneux, another suburb of Paris. On the night of January 20, 2006 he had what he thought was a date with an attractive blonde. In the event, she was fronting for a gang who called themselves "The Barbarians," and they abducted him. Most of them were extremist Muslims. Over three weeks, they tried to extort a ransom far beyond the means of his rather humble family, while at the same time torturing him. On several occasions, the gang telephoned the family and recited verses of the Qur'an to them while they could hear Halimi screaming in agony in the background. "They kept him naked and tied up," according to the police investigator, in whose opinion this was the cruellest killing he had ever come across, "They cut him and in the end poured flammable liquid on him and set him alight." On several previous occasions the gang had tried to kidnap other Jews, yet the Paris public prosecutor, Jean-Claude Marin, felt able to state, "no element of the current investigation could link this murder to an anti-Semitic declaration or action." Sarkozy was only one among others involved in the case to assert that the gang went for Halimi in the conviction that "the Jews have money."

The persistent refusal to treat facts for what they are raises the much larger issue of the differential attitude of the French elite towards Arabs and Jews. The recent insurgency is an outcome of the concept of France as *"une puissance musulmane,"* a concept which could only encourage Arabs and Muslims to feel entitled to make special demands on the country so eagerly co-opting and enrolling them into its national purposes. The definition of Jews as people who must abjure any distinguishing national identity, or else suffer the consequences for preserving their specificity, is one of those special demands, and it happens to coincide exactly with the statute put in place in 1789 by the Comte de Clermont-Tonnerre, and cherished by the state ever since.

Ideas and attitudes work downwards from the political elite that conceives them to the people who have to live with the consequences. The foreign ministry, generally referred to as the Quai d'Orsay, is the institution above all others responsible over an extended period of time for realising the state's grand design for Arabs and Jews and overseeing the political outcome that derives from it. The ministry's archives, along with the testimony of generations of diplomats, explain how a small number of highly motivated and carefully selected men of like mind have fostered the preconceptions of Arabs and Jews that have now come to threaten the integrity of the French nation.

TWO

The Quai d'Orsay

THE QUAI D'ORSAY occupies a splendid building in the opulent style of nineteenth-century Paris, next to the National Assembly on the left bank of the Seine. This, the architecture and the site proclaim, is where men of exceptional intelligence hold the nation's fate in their hands. French diplomats have often had literary gifts as well, which have qualified them at the end of a fulfilled career for election to the Académie Française. Many an insider's memoir has described the tea ceremony at five o'clock at which members of the Quai d'Orsay in its heyday used to gather and consolidate their thoughts. A huge literature written by diplomats harks back with nostalgia to the enduring club-like atmosphere of the place.

A few French foreign ministers have had the political skills to impose themselves and their policy objectives, in the manner of Théodore Delcassé and Raymond Poincaré. But the majority of them have come and gone with bewildering rapidity. Recurrent cabinet instability served to reinforce the scope and particularity of the Quai d'Orsay. Between September 1870 and August 1914, there were no less than thirty foreign ministers, and the turnover was as turbulent during the Fourth Republic, stabilizing only in today's Fifth Republic. Prime ministers have further devalued the position by often reserving it for themselves. Ministers have had to rely on their permanent civil servants, notably the secretary general, also referred to as Political Director, with overall charge of the ministry, the private cabinet at their disposal, and the heads of the various departments. Between 1870 and 1914 there were only thirteen Political Directors. By the close of the nineteenth century, France maintained just ten embassies, all in the capitals of the great powers. From 1900 to 1939, a total of only 89 ambassadors were nominated.

Self-selected members of the aristocracy staffed the ministry. All were required to have a private income of at least 6,000 francs a year. Competitive examination was introduced in 1894, but this and other reforms by and large served to perpetuate the ministry's good sense of itself, handed down by the old to the young. The expression *"la carrière"* has always been shorthand for being employed as a diplomat, as though there were no other career, just as *"ambassadeur de France"* is an irrevocable rank incorporating social and financial privileges. As a British diplomat attending the Paris Peace Conference at the end of the First War, Harold Nicolson was engaged in committee work at the Quai d'Orsay. Fascinated by coteries and the rites and rituals of power and exclusivity, his friend Marcel Proust cross-questioned him: "You climb the stairs. You go into the room. And then? Be specific, my friend, be specific."

In successive generations, the Cambons, Herbettes, Margeries, François-Poncets, and Courcels were nothing less than dynasties of diplomats. Gabriel Hanotaux, twice foreign minister towards the end of that century, and a prolific historian of France, rejoices in his autobiography *Mon Temps* that "The Department" formed "a sort of closed Academy." H. B. Haynes captures the mind-set of these men in his study *The French Foreign Office and the Origins of the First World War 1898–1914* (1993), writing that entry to the Quai d'Orsay at that period was determined by "nepotism, patronage, and political persuasion [which was] Catholic and hostile to Jews and Protestants and the parliamentary system."

THREE

Jews in the View of the Quai d'Orsay

IN DAMASCUS IN 1840 the rumor spread that Father Thomas, an Italian Capuchin friar, and his Arab servant had disappeared. The French consul, Comte Ulysse de Ratti-Menton, immediately accused the Jewish community of ritual murder. He persuaded the Ottoman governor to arrest a number of Jews and also hold Jewish children hostage. Some died under torture, others converted to Islam. Backing Ratti-Menton without reserve, Jean-Baptiste Beaudin, the dragoman and chancellor of the consulate, and two members of the consulate in Alexandria, Adrian-Louis Cochelet and Comte Maxime des Meloises, formed a self-supporting and insistent pressure group of officials on the spot.

In his book *The Damascus Affair*, Jonathan Frankel gives a masterly account of this scandal, which was to rock Europe. Adolphe Thiers, the Prime Minister, was too intelligent to believe the rehashed medieval myth that his agents were reporting, yet felt obliged, Frankel writes, to complain in the National Assembly that the Jews "are more powerful in the world than they have pretensions to be," and were putting forward their claims in every foreign chancellery. The real motive for not scotching the libel, Frankel suggests, was an opportunistic belief that France stood to gain advantage in the game of nations then playing out in the twilight of the Ottoman empire, and the rights and wrongs of the case were of no interest to Thiers, a consummate cynic. If so, here was a precedent that French diplomacy was to follow faithfully in the future. Ratti-Menton was unrepentant and the Quai d'Orsay defended him and his colleagues. The Arab media today like to depict ritual murder as a fact of Jewish life, and, whether they know it or not, they are rehearsing lessons learnt from French teachers long ago.

In October 1893, Paul Frédéric-Jean Grunebaum had an appointment at the Personnel Bureau of the Quai d'Orsay. The relevant document in the archives states, "M. Grunebaum is an Israelite: petitioning to be admitted on probation, he expressed the wish to know if this fact is of a kind to forbid him access to a diplomatic or consular career." The margin carries a minute from Louis Herbette, secretary general at the time. "I saw M. Grunebaum who spontaneously withdrew his request. He is indeed some-one distinguished and highly to be recommended. He bowed with good grace to the motives dictating the department's decision." At the time, Jews were alleged by the likes of Edouard Drumont and the Marquis de Morès to be secretly infiltrating French society at all levels, and to be resisted, or better still purged. As part of this campaign, a gazette with the title of *Indicateur Israélite* published in 1897 a list of the sixteen Jews who in the previous year were French consuls, in places ranging from Kansas City to Curaçao. A second list showed the twenty-two foreign Jews attached to their country's embassy or consulates. In October 1918, however, a magazine with the title *Pro-Israël* announced that the diplomatic service for the first time was open to a Jew, and a Monsieur Kahn had been nominated minister plenipotentiary in Siam.

Another revealing dossier contains letters written in 1895 by Paul Blanc, French consul at Canea in Crete, to Hanotaux, then Foreign Minister. Out on a shooting party, one of the guests, Mr. Almond, an Englishman, was suddenly taken ill and died. Two years later Blanc married Almond's widow. Madame de Schwartz, an elderly lady who had settled on the island, then published a pamphlet accusing Blanc of poisoning Almond. It was defense enough for Blanc to explain to Hanotaux that she was German-Jewish, conspiring with other Jews who by inference had to be in Ottoman pay.

J.-B. Barbier joined the diplomatic service in 1904, viewing it as the supreme refuge of "gallant men working for the French fatherland," and rose to be an ambassador. In his time, he comments in his memoirs *Un Frac de Nessus* (1951) "the career had no Jews among its members, at least as far as the important governing levels were concerned." Jews, he held, belonged to an "often parasitical ethnic element" and the way some did manage to penetrate senior levels was "disastrous." The Quai d'Orsay administered cultural programs through its

"Service des Œuvres françaises à l'étranger." In the 1930s, Jean Marx headed this service and J.-B. Barbier waged a passionate campaign against him as the epitome of the "anti-national Jew" who co-opted unreliable and even traitorous people of his own kind, duly backed by "International Jewry."

Anti-national was the euphemism for Jewish, and many applied it to Captain Alfred Dreyfus, the army officer falsely accused of betraying military secrets to the Germans. The conspiracy to find Dreyfus guilty of treason was hatched in the Ministry of War. The Quai d'Orsay as an institution accordingly stayed at a watchful distance. When the verdict of guilty was declared that December 1894, Foreign Minister Hanotaux told the German ambassador that the case was over, and he had no further right to raise it. Dreyfusards refused to let the injustice stand, and Anatole Catusse in Stockholm and Georges Bihourd in the Netherlands were among ambassadors lamenting the damage to France that the case was doing.

Maurice Paléologue had the duty of representing the ministry in 1899 at the appeal before the Cour de Cassation in Rennes, a safe distance from Paris. He saw the documents and met the officers who had forged the evidence, but this undoubtedly brilliant man was too slippery to be pinned down. When Madame Saint-René Taillandier, the wife of an eminent colleague, insisted to him that she believed in Dreyfus's innocence, he answered with an elusive negative: "I do not believe him guilty." Looking at Dreyfus's face as the verdict of reprieve approached, Paléologue thought he could detect in it a specifically Jewish trait down the ages, namely "an immense pride beneath a mask of humility." Fortunately, as he confided in a letter to Jusserand, who was to be ambassador in Washington for over twenty years, he himself was covered by an amnesty.

Few men placed a greater stamp on the Quai d'Orsay than Paul Cambon, born in 1843, and his brother Jules, two years younger. Both were powerful personalities at the heart of the cosmopolitan diplomacy of their day. Paul Cambon was ambassador in London for twenty-two years, and a principal architect of the Entente Cordiale with Britain, while Jules was ambassador in Washington for seven years before Jusserand. Both were involved with Arab affairs, Paul as Resident in Tunisia, Jules as Governor-General of Algeria. Paul Cambon believed that Dreyfus as a Jew was a traitor by definition, and he changed his mind only once the appeal process had started. This most sophisticated man, in command of the widest available access to information, in a letter dated March 19, 1900 could point an accusing finger at "the prodigious international influence of the Jews; they are masters of peace and war." In common with many colleagues, his brother Jules persisted in thinking Dreyfus guilty to the end. Auguste Gérard, another ambassador, summed up in his *Mémoires* the attitude of all those unable to abandon their prejudices. The anti-Dreyfusards, he thought, were the "natural defenders" of the nation and its nationality, the "true representatives of France and its genius."

Pogroms in Czarist Russia were occurring at the same

time as the Dreyfus trial. Maurice Bompard, ambassador in St. Petersburg from 1902 to 1908 and a man much esteemed by his colleagues, wrote in a report in August 1903: "I pass over in silence anti-Jewish disturbances such as those in Kishinev because they are, so to speak, on the rebound from agrarian disturbances. The Jewish population, so badly treated in Russia, engaged in perpetual hostilities with the Russian authorities, is a nursery of nihilists and agitators." Just one year later, writing to Foreign Minister Delcassé, he compared the "wise and calm Finns" to the Jews, "detested but indispensable at the same time, themselves full of hatred as they hold the people to ransom and undermine authority."

In due course Paléologue succeeded Bompard at St. Petersburg, and he was to write diaries and books with important first-hand testimony about the end of Czarism and the Bolshevik revolution. Czarist policy towards the Jews, he said, seemed devised to sustain "their hereditary defects and their bad passions, to exasperate their hatred for Goyim, to plunge them deeper into their Talmudic prejudices, to affirm them in their state of permanent inner rebellion, to bring the indestructible hope of promised reparations shining in their eyes.... The vengeful and vindictive stubbornness of the Jews could not have found a more favorable climate." In 1915 he could send this laconic telegram: "Since the beginning of the war Russian Jews have not had to submit to any collective violence.... In the zone of operations a few hundred Jews have been hanged for espionage: nothing more."

FOUR

The Catholic Factor

IN THE LATTER PART of the nineteenth century, the French built up their position simultaneously in North Africa and in the Ottoman provinces comprising Syria, Lebanon, and what Europeans then generally called the Holy Land. In the latter case, the process was slow and piecemeal, often promoted by pious and rich individuals. Comte Paul de Piellat, for instance, settled in Jerusalem, purchased real estate including the site where Saint Peter supposedly heard the cock crowing, and endowed the Catholic Church with it. The French had hospitals in Jerusalem, Bethlehem, Nazareth, and Nablus; monasteries and seminaries and several churches including one at Abu Ghosh that the Sultan had specially granted them; they owned and operated the Jerusalem-Jaffa railway. According to one authority, Pierre Guillen, 5,000 French schools in the Levant had 80,000 pupils. Another authority, however, Jacques Thobie, estimates that by the outbreak of the First War the maximum number of actual French citizens living in the Holy Land was 150 to 200. The Crédit Lyonnais opened a branch in Jerusalem in 1895, and Thobie quotes one of its inspectors complaining that the city "is a tomb in which you die of boredom."

In 1888 the Vatican decreed that Catholics and Catholic institutions should look for protection exclusively to France. Jules Ferry, most imperial of French politicians, held that "This protectorate of Christians in the Orient is in some sense part of our Mediterranean domain," offering "a serious tradition, a moral power." Aspiring to counteract the British then consolidating their hold on Egypt, Gabriel Hanotaux believed that through its Catholic protectorate France was the only European power "capable of acting without fatal contention but side by side with Muslim monotheism."

The anti-clericalism of the Left, and France's break with the Vatican, cut right across any such claim to tradition and moral power. The government for instance attacked Notre Dame, the most prominent French monastery in Jerusalem, for its continued opposition to Dreyfus after his innocence had been established. At the same time, Germany, Italy, and Russia were all paying France the compliment of imitating its policy of expansion by means of the worshippers and institutions belonging to their respective religions. Kaiser Wilhelm's visit to the Holy Land in 1898 was an open challenge on these lines. German and French Benedictines were at odds with one another in Jerusalem. Treaties in 1901 and 1913 with first the Sultan and then the Young Turks protected France's privileged position in the Holy Land, and appeared to be building blocks towards the desired goal of becoming a true *"puissance musulmane."*

A Comité de l'Asie française was founded in 1901, and eight years later a second Comité des Intérêts français en Orient was given the purpose of developing "our moral, economic, and political standing in the Orient." Its board included a former prime minister A. Ribot, and President Raymond Poincaré. An official, Maurice Pernot, was commissioned to visit various Turkish provinces in 1912, and as a result of his report the committees were amalgamated in order to extend France's religious protectorate in political and economic directions.

FIVE

Zionism versus French Designs

THE RISE OF political Zionism on the international scene promised to bestow a modern national identity on Jews, and this would altogether overturn the French state's insistent definition of who they were and what their place was. French diplomats in central and eastern Europe were quick to register dismay, and search for open or occult causes for this unwelcome development. Writing from the Legation in Bucharest in June 1902, L. Descoy described the arrival in the city of Bernard Lazare, the gifted Jewish polemicist, and an early Zionist. The "extreme enthusiasm" of the Jewish community, he thought, was whipped up by the newspaper *Adevarul* "whose leading editors are Israelites," which brought into play the otherwise feeble group representing Romanian opinion and encouraged anti-French sentiments at large. In Budapest, Vicomte de Fontenay, in charge of the Consulate, in August 1906 reported that the appearance of Zionism was for the Magyar population quite understandably "a new cloud," likely to "become worse with time."

According to rumor, the Young Turks now in power were secret Jews and Freemasons. In February 1911, Max Chouttier, Consul in Salonika, reported articles against Zionism in the official press, giving his own opinion that these warnings "should be of a kind to give the Jewish communities pause for thought and encourage them to oppose Germano-Zionist propaganda."

G. Deville, the minister in Athens, was asked to comment on a memorandum concerning the role in Salonika of the Alliance Israélite universelle, the school system set up by French Jews to promote Jewish education and culture in the Middle East. To Deville, the Alliance screened its true ambitions. Its Parisian director "might be a good Frenchman, but those of his religion in Salonika think only of serving themselves and not of serving France: if they study and spread French, it is only because French is still, except for a few idioms, the most useful medium of general commerce in the Levant. In these circumstances, is it to our benefit to upset the Greeks in order to flatter Jewish pride?" In *Le Mirage Oriental* (1910), Louis Bertrand, another polished writer-diplomat, published an account of his visit to Ottoman Palestine. In a chapter with the telling title of "La Déplaisance du Juif," he maintained that Sephardi Jews were in fact an aristocracy among the otherwise displeasing people he met in "their hybrid clothes, half European, half Oriental, dirty, with glowering looks ... hordes crazed with poverty and mysticism."

Confession d'un vieux diplomate (1953), by the Comte de Saint-Aulaire, similarly loses no chance to disparage any Jews encountered in a long career. Moroccans were right to pillage the Jewish quarter, this veteran of the Quai d'Orsay thought, because the Jews were "leeches" gorging at their expense. To him, the Russian press at the time of the revolution was in the hands of Jews and Germanophiles, the capital of Hungary was "Yudapesth," Léon Blum was a German agent, and, perhaps most fantastically of all, Arthur Balfour, the British foreign secretary and renowned Zionist, is alleged to have told him that in any National Home Jews would live off rich Jews abroad in the manner of parasites.

From the London embassy Paul Cambon in October 1912 wrote to his brother Jules about "the anti-Russian agitation now being spread everywhere by the Jews." He linked together some sort of invisible intrigue between a Catholic paper, *Le Correspondant,* the polemicist Lucien Wolf, admittedly "a talented German Jew," and the press in Vienna, "where we know that the papers are in the hands of Jews." In April 1913, still writing to his brother, he described how he had received "an Israelo-Macedonian committee," which was lobbying for an autonomous Macedonia. This was yet another consequence of the Young Turks revolution, which "has been organized, paid for, and kept going by the Jews or by Jews of Muslim origins and all of them affiliated to Freemasonry."

In the Holy Land itself, Zionism had implications far greater than it did in Europe, for it was by definition a competitor to French expansionism and France's Catholic protectorate. The spontaneous reaction was two-fold: to heap contempt on Zionism and to sponsor Arab nationalism in opposition to it. Najib Azoury, a Maronite from Beirut, had been employed in the Ottoman bureaucracy in Jerusalem. In mysterious circumstances he fled to Cairo, was tried in absentia, sentenced to death, and moved on to Paris. There he published a booklet, *Le Réveil de la Nation arabe*, predicting that Jews and Arabs were destined to fight until one eliminated the other. The Quai d'Orsay apparently subsidized *L'Indépendance arabe*, a journal he began to write and put out in 1907. Paying for the meeting in Paris in June 1913 of twenty-three Arabs from Syria and the Holy Land, the Quai d'Orsay effectively launched the Arab nationalist movement.

The First War heralded the long-predicted demise of the Ottoman empire. Two highly restricted groups of specialists handled the political consequences that followed the redrawing of the Middle East map: the men in the Quai d'Orsay's "*direction politique*" and the "*sous-direction de l'Asie*," and the members of the two committees already representing colonial interests, the Comité de l'Asie and the Comité de l'Orient. The personnel overlapped. Philippe Berthelot, at the time Political Director of the Quai d'Orsay, and his energetic general secretary Robert de Caix, Jean Gout, François Georges-Picot, Bruno de Margerie, and others from the ministry were also members of the Comité de l'Asie. Men of intellect and experience, undoubtedly patriots, they were of one mind: France already controlled the Arab western shores of the Mediterranean, and now could add the eastern shores, or what these experts referred to as "*la Syrie intégrale*," that is, Syria, Lebanon, and the Holy Land. The question before them was how to utilize either Arab nationalism or Zionism to their purposes.

Georges-Picot was Councilor at the French embassy in London. In secret inter-government negotiations in 1916 with Sir Mark Sykes, a Conservative member of Parliament, he believed that agreement had been reached which granted France possession of "*la Syrie intégrale*." According to Georges-Picot, "ninety-five per cent of the French people strongly favored the annexation of Palestine by France." The Germans, it was suspected, were about to issue a proclamation of support for Zionism, and this would swing Russian Jews to their side and have a bearing on the outcome of the war. American Jews were thought to have a comparable influence. André Tardieu, French high commissioner in America, a future member of the Council of Ten at Versailles and a future prime minister and foreign minister as well, wrote to his Foreign Minister Stephen Pichon that the right of Jews to self-determination should be taken into consideration for fear that "certain elements in American Jewry" might otherwise lose interest in recovering Alsace and Lorraine for France. American Jewry, then, was presented holding France's post-war fate in its hands (M.A.E.–C.P.C./ A-Guerre 1914–1918/Vol. 120).

Jean Gout was head of the Asian Section with responsibility for the Ottoman provinces and their fate. On May 7, 1917, he sent a memorandum to Clemenceau via Margerie, his *chef de cabinet.* "The millenarian hopes of the Jews, especially the proletarians of Poland and Russia, are not socialist as their social standing might suggest, nor national as the declarations of their intellectuals pretend, but they are essentially Talmudic, that is to say religious. These poor devils have been nurtured on myths of misery which gives them a glimpse of Jerusalem as the end of their ills. . . . Even intelligent and educated Jews who have come to the top in countries with equal opportunities cherish for generations in a corner of their heart the dream of the old ghettoes. Thanks to their wealth and the links they preserve between themselves, and the pressure they exert on ignorant governments, they represent an international value [*une valeur internationale*]."

An earlier proposal to create a small autonomous Jewish state with Hebron as its capital and Gaza as its port had prompted Jules Cambon to minute: "They could grow oranges and exploit each other." But since the powers were one and all bidding for Jewish favors, the French could do so too, and in June 1917 Cambon wrote a letter to the Zionist leadership to assure French support "in the renaissance of the Jewish nationality in that land from which the people of Israel were exiled so long ago." At the time, the letter was not released for publication, and it was no sooner sent than regretted as the Quai d'Orsay returned to its habitual anxiety on the subject, circulating anti-Zionist memoranda and bombarding the British with demands to abstain from any action that might raise unrealizable Jewish hopes.

That November, the British foreign secretary Arthur

Balfour issued the declaration named after him in favor of "a national home for the Jewish people," something far more supportive of Zionism than Cambon's letter. The British government felt able to propose and dispose —it had 150,000 soldiers fighting the Turks, while the French had 800, with some further irregulars. On Christmas Day 1917, Field Marshal Allenby entered the city of Jerusalem with Georges-Picot in the entourage. Two days later at a picnic, the latter suggested setting up the civil administration he thought he had negotiated with Sykes. Also present was Lawrence of Arabia, and his description of Allenby's scornful response is one of the most famous passages in *Seven Pillars of Wisdom*.

A. de Fleuriau, Councilor in the embassy in London, reported to Pichon on December 27, 1917 that Jewish intellectuals from London University were largely responsible for Zionism, and they had courted the votes of poor Jews. The children of the latter, however, had almost all forsaken their religion, and they were anti-militaristic, "their atavism not preparing them for the profession of bearing arms." Two days later he amplified this, writing that rich Jews were hostile to the Balfour Declaration, but the opinion enthusiastically expressed by poor Jews and immigrants was that "The Israelite race was superior to all others; it possessed colonies in all the countries and one day it shall dominate the world."

An unsigned position paper in the archives (M.A.E.-C.P.C.P.C/E-Levant/Palestine/1918–1940/Vol. 12) has the title "The Jewish Question and Zionism." The author posits that Zionism corresponds to the mysticism of Russian-Polish Ashkenazis. The movement's propagandists had spread their nefarious ideas to other Jews in Algeria and Morocco, trying to enroll and organize them. "This propaganda is all the more dangerous in that it seeks to exploit great power rivalry." The Spanish government was already asserting special claims over the Sephardi Jews in the French possessions of North Africa. The author had some classic advice: "Our Jewish policy in North Africa is necessarily linked to our Muslim policy, we have to avoid Jewish nationalism as also Pan-Islamism or Pan-Arabism, by favoring a slow and careful evolution in the direction of our civilization."

On January 15, 1919, Foreign Minister Stephen Pichon instructed de Fleuriau's ambassador Paul Cambon to draw to the British government's attention that Zionist propaganda should not be allowed to become a cause for trouble in the Middle East. "The Allied authorities should abstain from all actions or declarations which might arouse unrealizable expectations in the Jews. . . . The Zionists must understand once and for all that there could be no question of constituting an independent Jewish state in Palestine, nor even forming some sovereign Jewish body [*organisme*]." Three days later Cambon wrote to Pichon that he could hardly believe the conversation he had just had with Balfour. In his usual dilettante and eclectic manner, Balfour had said that, "it would be interesting to be present at the reconstitution of the Kingdom of Jerusalem." Cambon replied that according

35

to the Apocalypse such a reconstitution would signal the end of the world. Balfour came back: "It would be still more interesting to be present at the end of the world."

SIX

Between the Wars

THE POST-WAR TREATY of peace signed at Sèvres settled the disposition of the former Ottoman provinces. France was to have a mandate for Syria, but not Greater Syria (*"la Syrie intégrale"*) because Palestine was incorporated into a British mandate. The British were Christians where the Ottomans had been Muslims, and France duly renounced the letter of its Catholic protectorate, but not the spirit. A Catholic paper, *L'Œuvre d'Orient*, wrote, "It is inadmissible that the 'Country of Christ' should become the prey of Jewry and of Anglo-Saxon heresy. It must remain the inviolable inheritance of France and the Church. It would be a national infamy and an irreparable crime not to remove this sacred land from the brutal rapacity of our allies. Divine punishment would be swift to follow and the Catholic world would curse us for it" (quoted in Christopher M. Andrew and A. S. Kanya-Forstner, *France Overseas*). The Quai d'Orsay never ceased to play one side off against the other at every level. The legation in Guatemala, for instance, reported on August 16, 1919, that Miguel Aboularach, a dignitary from the local Syrian community, was about to return to his home in Bethlehem. He was a member of the Anti-Zionist Association of New York, and as the legation put it, "in that respect he might be listened to with interest."

British troops withdrew from Syria, and General Henri Gouraud arrived in Damascus in October 1919 to take up his appointment as French High Commissioner. A former collaborator with Marshal Lyautey in Morocco and recently a successful commander on the Western front, he believed in France's colonial mission. His secretary general, Robert de Caix, was also French Representative at the Permanent Mandates Commission in Geneva from 1923 to 1939, and one authority, Peter A. Shambrook, describes him as the *éminence grise* at the Quai d'Orsay on the Levant question. In the ministry's classic manner, he favored a policy of playing the region's minorities off against each other in the interests of French supremacy. A minuscule number of Arab nationalists were prepared to resist the French mandate, and they were scattered peremptorily by French troops and Moroccan auxiliaries in a skirmish at Maysalun close to Damascus.

Already in November, Georges-Picot on a visit was sending a telegram to the Quai d'Orsay to specify that the British authorities in Jerusalem were at last becoming aware of growing Muslim discontent with the Jews, and this "could only be to the benefit of our influence." During the first six months of 1920, Gouraud bombarded the office with anti-Zionist telegrams. Muslims and Christians were expecting conditions to be worse than under the Turks, he wrote; the Zionists, "recruited from the whole world over," would not respect minority rights, but impose their language and resort to clever tricks ("*habiles mesures*") of eviction to gain access to official jobs with the help of local government. A firmer Catholic protectorate was required. "No doubt we should take advantage of circumstances to enlarge the scope of this protectorate and extend it to the Muslims whom we cannot leave alone and unarmed to face Zionism." A telegram of February 18, 1920 states outright that Palestine would gain from the guardianship of France. A year later, in July 1921, he recommended that Prime Minister Aristide Briand receive Salha Bey Al-Husseini of the Palestine National Council, who was in Paris to protest against the Jewish home.

The boundary between the French and British mandates remained uncertain, and one of de Caix's first duties was to travel to Jerusalem to discuss the issue with Sir Herbert Samuel, the British High Commissioner. In a preliminary letter dated October 19, 1920, de Caix unfolded what was already political orthodoxy in his circle, namely that the British and the Jews were conspiring together against French interests. From the outset he felt personally slighted, feeling that he had been received in a rather mediocre way ("*assez médiocrement reçu*"). Samuel, he explained, "represents in Palestine what it is appropriate to call Anglo-Jewish policy. This well-mannered English Jew, scraped clean from the ghetto (*"décrassé des ghettos"*), has been completely taken up in Jerusalem by his tribe and he attends synagogue, accepts no invitations on the Sabbath and on Holy Days goes only on foot. It is a strange phenomenon when one reflects on the evident ignominy of Jews from Galicia and other surrounding regions who are now flooding Palestine but constrain people like Sir Herbert into their mummery. Before doing anything worthwhile in the country, these people dream of spreading at our expense, and you may be sure that the complete Jewry of both hemispheres will apply a policy consisting of rejecting our frontier to the north of the Hauran and to the banks of the Litani."

In his lengthy final report, de Caix referred to what he took as another personal insult, this time because Samuel had refused an invitation to dine at the French consulate on the grounds that it was the Sabbath. British policy, de Caix elaborated, may have sought to exploit Jewish strength against France, but was in fact largely exploited by it. Jews had infiltrated the administration, and British officials were either careful not to oppose Zionism, or left the country in disgust. Religion for the Jews was only a means to an end, "all are animated by passionate nationalism and a thirst for revenge." They would prove harmful neighbors: "The frequent revolutionary and prophetic spirit of the Jews derives from the Bolshevism of the colonists eastern Europe is sending to Palestine. Through conviction, and also through the instinctive tendency to fragment societies whose cohesion might stand in the way of their expansion, these people will make propaganda in Lebanon and Syria. They will try to break the traditional framework of religious confessions already threatened for other reasons."

British dominion, de Caix concluded, was a kind of despoiling which had occurred only because the French had sacrificed themselves for the Allied cause on the Western front. The French language and French intellectual influence were paramount. Evidence that the Western presence in Jerusalem took a French form, he thought worth emphasizing, lay in the principal door of the Church of the Holy Sepulchre, "in the solid and massive ogival style born in the twelfth century in the Ile de France." Zionists ignored the role that Jerusalem had played in the history of humanity. He consoled himself finally with the thought that the future of Zionism remained doubtful. More than any other race, he wrote, the Jews had lost the habit of agriculture. Their colonization was artificial, expensive, and divisive. "If under the British mandate the native population has a tendency to react, there is every chance that they will try to maintain, as indeed they do in Egypt, the French culture which retains such attraction."

On November 3, Gouraud forwarded to Paris what he rightly called "this remarkable report," adding his opinion that Zionism was a threat to Syria (M.A.E.-C.P.C./ E-Levant/Palestine/1918–1929/Vol. 3). The loss of the Catholic protectorate made the protection of French institutions more essential than ever, as they were "the bastion of our influence." Twelve days later, Georges-

Picot in a telegram from Beirut informed the ministry that the British authorities in Jerusalem were taking precautions against riots, and warning Muslims that they, the Muslims, would be responsible for any disorder. "This attitude can only benefit our influence, as irritation with Zionism is only growing among Syrian Muslims." The consuls in mandatory Palestine were increasingly alarmist. Durieux in Haifa reported in March 1921 that the government was recruiting unemployed Jews as the core of a future Jewish army, and that Jewish and Protestant elements were cutting away the ground under the Catholics—that is to say, France. That May, Durieux opened another report on riots during the previous days in Jaffa with the terse sentence, "No change today, extreme over-excitement, few dead and wounded." But at least, "Our car was borne in triumph by the population crying Long Live France, down with the Jews."

At that same moment, de Caix was forwarding to Aristide Briand, then foreign Minister, extracts from the *Protocols of the Elders of Zion*, which, he stated as fact, had been "secretly communicated to some Jews highly placed in Palestine." It was not possible for him to guarantee the authenticity of the enclosed document, he explained in a sentence revealing his belief in conspiracy, but it could be linked to information the department had received a few years earlier "on the subject of the preparation in the United States of the bolshevik movement, whose trace it might be possible to recover" (M.A.E.-C.P.C/E-Levant/Palestine/1918–1929/ Vol. 15).

De Caix's wholly fanciful interpretation of Zionism had a lasting impact on the Quai d'Orsay. Reports from North Africa confirmed rising alarmism. Marshal Lyautey in the French Protectorate of Morocco was perhaps the most influential and respected spokesman for old-style French imperialism. In a note dated June 8, 1923 (M.A.E.-C.P.C./E-Levant/Palestine/1918–1940/Vol. 51), he reiterated what was already the standard argument that Zionism had no authenticity of its own, and he took credit for advising caution towards it. "This caution is understandable: of foreign inspiration, receiving its directives from abroad, serving principally the interests of a determined power, Zionism constitutes a doctrine whose importation into Morocco is hardly to be desired, and which in any case the Protectorate should not favor."

Typically seeking to show that Jews were not what they might seem to be, an unsigned report dated December 2, 1925 (M.A.E-C.P.C/E. Levant/Palestine/1918–1940/Vol. 28) drew further attention to the *Protocols of the Elders of Zion*. Although this forgery purporting to be evidence of a Jewish conspiracy to take over the world had by then been exposed, the author gives credence to "facts" which are "inexplicable" and concludes that, if the matter is to be taken seriously, "we have to deal with a really diabolical plan."

That same year, Panafieu, ambassador in Warsaw, reported that the Zionist conference held in that city was an abuse of the government's liberal policy and an appeal for privilege. Jews were unwilling to accept any idea of Polish nationality, or even simple loyalty: "It is not surprising that the violent proposals so noisily put forward here are received unfavorably by public opinion." Covering another Zionist congress in Cracow ten years later, J. Laroche, the succeeding ambassador to Poland, had developed the critique to suit changing times: "Basing themselves on conceptions which are more racial than religious, they aspire to set up on both banks of the Jordan a Jewish state conceived on the fascist model." This ambassador seems to have been among the very first to draw a parallel between Zionism and Nazism, going so far as to write that the Revisionist Zionist Vladimir Jabotinsky was the Chief to his followers, exactly as Hitler was the "Führer" in Germany.

First-hand experience of the Palestine mandate occasionally disposed an official to a favorable view of Zionism. One such was Henry de Jouvenel, Gouraud's successor as High Commissioner in Syria. He visited Jerusalem in 1926, and afterwards wrote, "Anti-Zionist when I arrived in the East, I became Zionist, or rather jealous of the British High Commissioner in Palestine and all that the Zionists contribute." Naturally France was obligated to support the Christians, but the Jews helped themselves, and he admired their spirit of enterprise.

There were also realists like Philippe Berthelot, secretary general from 1920 to 1933. As he commented at the outset of his stint, "Zionism is a fact." His regret was that the Jews of England had understood the Zionist mission, while French Jews had proved unable to take "the lead of world Jewry to the benefit of France." At his instigation, the Quai d'Orsay towards the end of 1925 set up a special department for religious affairs under Louis Canet. In the words of one historian, this was the obligatory antechamber for visiting Zionist leaders as well as representatives of the Catholic orders in mandatory Palestine. After a meeting in the office with Chaim Weizmann in May 1927, Canet concluded a memorandum with a clear expression of his inner thoughts: "Jewish nationalism is a mistake and Israel [i.e., Jews] can find peace only through assimilation."

* * *

In the years between 1919 and 1940 there were fourteen Ministers of Foreign Affairs in forty-one governments, a turnover in part responsible for France's inability to take the measure of the period's ominous upheavals. As the Second World War approached, writes one specialist, "the direction given to the Quai d'Orsay was simply non-existent." The ministry sought refuge in continuity. Berthelot fell into disgrace through association with a dubious financial consortium in China, but he and Alexis Saint-Léger, his successor as secretary general, were extremely capable. So were André François-Poncet and Robert Coulondre, successively ambassadors in Berlin. Yet they and the Third Republic politicians whom they served sought the shelter of the status quo, even though this meant appeasing the strong at the expense of the weak. All of a kind, their background and temperament conditioned them. Each year in the Thirties the number of recruits was almost invariably limited to low single figures. Groomed in the select higher schools, candidates were examined in history, international and civil law, economic geography, and they were required to know two foreign languages. A committee of four senior diplomats further vetted the candidates to ensure that they were socially and culturally presentable. In 1935, "the Career" comprised just 191 diplomats, only one of them a woman, while the subordinate consular service employed 398 men. Here was a prime example of a French institution unable to take the measure of the Age of the Dictators. The policy of appeasement favored at that time by the British Foreign Office reflects a comparably narrow mentality and lack of imagination.

The knowledge that Jews were trying to escape from Europe to Palestine, the French authorities feared, would provoke violence in Muslim countries under French rule, and especially Syria. As from March 1933, Jewish travelers were allowed to enter Syria only on condition that they had obtained immigration visas to Palestine from a British consulate abroad. That October, official measures to help German-Jewish refugees in France were suspended. An unsigned note of March 27, 1934 (M.A.E.-C.P.C./E–Levant/Palestine/1918–1940/Vol. 65) from the Contrôle des Étrangers section of the Direction des Affaires Politiques to the Minister states that a group of German Jews intending to promote Zionism should be refused entry. Zionists were finding "ingenious methods and fanciful motives ... to evade current regulations."

Henri Gaillard, consul in Cairo, on 21 March 1934 thought that the Jews of Egypt had been clumsy as a result of events in Palestine and Hitler's policy in Germany: "Complaining without limit about the fate of those who share their religion and displaying exaggerated appetites, they have succeeded in creating a strong current of Arab opinion against themselves, in this country where until now their position was completely privileged." Gaston Bernard, consul in Trieste, on February 4, 1935 reported that his city was profiting from Jewish emigration to Palestine. On the Lloyd Triestino steamships involved, "Care has been carried to the extreme of ensuring that the emigrants have services of the Talmudic cult and the exclusive use of Kosher cuisine: and this, it has to be said, communicates a *sui generis* odor to these ships which customers of a normal composition no doubt would appreciate less highly."

In the immediate aftermath of Hitler's invasion of Austria in March 1938, the American government invited twenty-eight European and Latin American governments to a conference at Evian, in order to discuss how to facilitate the emigration of political refugees. By tacit agreement, and ostensibly for fear of stoking anti-Semitism, there was no open reference to Jews. Nothing of substance was agreed at what has been called "the Jewish Munich." In the judgment of one authority, Catherine Nicault, "the absolute lack of generosity in French policy is less striking than the indifference towards even keeping up any appearance of it," and she notes in support of this condemnation the frequency of anti-Semitic propositions on the part of French officials.

After the collapse of France as a result of Hitler's blitzkrieg, Marshal Pétain agreed to an armistice in June 1940, and then formed his Vichy government with the intention of collaborating with Nazi Germany. Escaping to England at that same moment, General de Gaulle displayed a determination to resist so far removed from the official response that it was quixotic. According to André Gillois in his *Histoire secrète des Français à Londres de 1940 à 1944*, the French embassy in London advised a Gaullist-minded journalist, "Don't go over to them, they're Communists and Jews." That October, without any prompting from Hitler, Vichy passed the Statut des Juifs, its version of the Nuremberg Laws in force in Germany excluding Jews from whole areas of public life. Jacques Guérard was the *directeur du Cabinet* of Paul Baudoin, then the foreign minister, and he sent a telegram to the ambassador in Washington, Gaston Henry-Haye, forwarding arguments he hoped would settle any disquiet about this statute in American public opinion. The pre-war Left, the telegram averred in defiance of the facts, had allowed Jews to enter the country in hundreds of thousands. These Jews, with "their special mentality" had attacked "all the ideas from which the French had never wavered." At a time when Guérard knew that dispossession and arrests were already the order of the day, he went on, "No measure has been taken against individuals or property." The purpose of the statute, he concluded, was "to allow the peaceful existence in France of elements whose racial characteristics make them dangerous when they mix too intimately with our political and administrative life."

Collaboration and a genuine foreign policy were incompatible. Saint-Léger left for New York. Ambassadors in important capitals like François-Poncet, Charles Corbin, Léon Noel, and François Charles-Roux resigned. Some diplomats obeyed Vichy instructions, however. On July 4, 1941, Robert de Margerie, consul general in Shanghai, sent Admiral de la Flotte, a member of Pétain's cabinet and Secretary of State in the Ministry of Foreign Affairs, a list of French civilians, sailors, and soldiers who had left Shanghai in order, as he put it, "to reach England or a colony of the British embassy with a view to joining up with dissident forces." After the German take-over of the Vichy zone in November 1942, Jean Chauvel, René Massigli, Louis de Guiringaud, and some twenty others resigned; some escaped into Spain and then on to Algiers or London. A list put together in Vichy on February 20, 1943 shows that the general secretary was Charles Rochat, with a tiny handful of men under him. Asked later by Chauvel why he didn't resign, Rochat answered that he was maintaining "the continuous affirmation of French sovereignty." This was illusory: the Quai d'Orsay had virtually ceased to function.

SEVEN

Writers Take Sides

In his years as secretary general (1920–21, 1925–32), Philippe Berthelot set a special tone of exclusivity and dilettantism to which many of those who served under him have paid tribute in print. The son of a celebrated industrial chemist, Berthelot had supreme self-confidence and application, wide social connections, and genuine literary tastes. He invited the disgraced Oscar Wilde to regular lunches, and was one of the nine people present at Wilde's funeral in Paris. His wife, Hélène, had a fashionable salon. Under his sponsorship and protection, Paul Morand, Paul Claudel, Jean Giraudoux, and others were given the time and the security which enabled them to build international literary reputations, as though they were members of an elite club rather than an institution of government. (Jules Cambon is supposed to have summed up the prevailing attitude to office hours: "Come in as late as you like, but no later"). Berthelot's successor as secretary general was Alexis

Saint-Léger, an elusive personality and poet from the French West Indies who under the pseudonym of St.-John Perse was to win the Nobel Prize. Taken together, these men perpetuated the image of the Quai d'Orsay as the repository of a culture and brilliance generally accepted as pre-eminent.

Paul Morand had grown up in an artistic milieu. At the age of 25, he passed top into the Quai d'Orsay in the exams of 1913. Among his early writings is *Mort d'un Juif* in which a Jew on his death-bed refuses to pay the doctor until the rate of exchange has improved. In *Mort d'un autre Juif*, the dying victim of a pogrom feels that he has been "faithful to the truth under the mask of eternal treason." For Morand, as the critic Jean-François Fogel puts in his book *Morand-Express*, "cupidity or treason" are the two life-choices facing Jews. Alexis Saint-Léger wrote to Morand, "You have a prodigious gift." Berthelot expected great things of Morand, who in turn described him as a "seigneur." In his *Journal d'un attaché d'ambassade* he recorded how Berthelot had received the news in 1917 that the Bolsheviks had seized the Tauride palace and expelled the Duma. This would all end in sharing land and massacring the Jews, said Berthelot, "which is after all not a bad program." Morand commented that the cynicism was a cover: "here is humor at the service of firmness."

Morand used his status as a diplomat to travel with privilege all over the world. In 1927 he married the Romanian Hélène Chrisoveleni, divorced wife of Prince Dimitry Soutzo, Romanian military attaché in Paris, and they settled smoothly into the beau monde of one capital city after another. His many books display know-all cosmopolitan superiority, verging on flippancy and time and again resorting to malicious descriptions of Jews. In *New York* (1930), for example, he says that the city's Jewish literature has a spiritual tension and an abstract quality explicable because East Side Jews have never seen a tree. They are "preachers, self-immolators, socialists, anarchists, Bolsheviks, communists and others 'ists' perpetually quarrelling and cursing each other," altogether "giving a rather exact idea of what Jerusalem must have been." Local cinemas were showing a Soviet film, and "The chosen people is queuing to see the boyars (it's their turn at last) get a kick in the pants. . . . *Alles gut!*" The sight of Delancey Street prompted this typical reaction: "Grilled and salted almonds are sold by peddlers whose frozen hooked noses stick out of a moth-eaten fur cap brought over from Russia by the ancestors. In shop-windows are huge gilded carp, sweet pickled cucumbers, ritual poultry and kosher meat with its internal hemorrhaging, those special sausages like huge blood-clotted members, not to mention the minces and oriental dishes looking like excrement."

Morand claimed that his novel *France la Doulce* (1934) was comedy, a satire. True, he was not Céline calling outright for the massacre of Jews, but this novel has a central place in the anti-Semitic literature of the period. Its theme is that Jews control the cinema, making films with the single objective of money-grubbing, and so debauching public taste. Its sole French character turns out to be a Jew passing himself off under a false identity. In the course of a journey to India in 1935, Morand traveled through the Middle East. Syria, he thought, was slipping from French hands while the Jews were cultivating their fields with rifles on their shoulders, in "an alliance of earth and blood without which there is no real country"—the phrase has a Hitlerian ring.

In 1940 Morand was in London at the head of an economic warfare mission. Like all but a handful of the eight hundred French officials in Britain at the collapse of France, he rejected de Gaulle's appeal to join the Free French and returned home. In Vichy he applied for a job, and in view of his novel about the Jewish stranglehold on the cinema in due course was made President of the Commission for Film Censorship. He lived mostly in Paris, where his wife entertained on a considerable scale, warning her French guests that after six o'clock German guests would arrive. To the end, she liked to declare that she was a Nazi and would always be one. In 1943 Morand took up the appointment of French ambassador in Bucharest, and for a few weeks before the end of Vichy the following year he was ambassador in Berne. He and his wife judged it prudent to stay in Switzerland while there was any chance of recrimination. In 1958 de Gaulle himself vetoed Morand's election to the Académie Française, only to consent to it ten years later. Such a reversal of judgment on those who had morally compromised themselves was by then standard practice, and it served to embellish Morand's acceptance of fascism into another facet of a lifelong dandyism.

Jean Giraudoux was among Morand's closest friends and colleagues. He liked to stress that both his parents were from the Limousin, that is to say French from deepest France. He knew England and America well, and spoke English fluently. An aesthete, he wrote in a style that was elegant and subtle, suffused with irony. Claudel was among the first to praise him. One of his novels gave an affectionate portrait of the large and well-connected Berthelot family, including his superior. Yet he litters his work with aspersions and stereotypes, as when he has a Jewish character in *Siegfried et le limousin* say, "The beak of the German eagle is our nose." In 1939 he published an autobiographical book *De Pleins Pouvoirs à Sans Pouvoirs,* depicting how at that critical moment he had been in the habit of escaping to his office in the Quai d'Orsay, "the sole refuge where, just as nobody spoke of war in the trenches, I could at last exchange ideas on the size of poodles and the framing of Daumiers." That August, on the eve of war, he was appointed to run the Commissariat à l'Information, supposedly the opposite number to Goebbels though in fact complementing the latter's racial opinions. In *Pleins Pouvoirs* he stated that only the French race could save the country, "and we are in complete agreement with Hitler in proclaiming that policy attains its superior form only when it is racial." As for Jews, he had been taken to meet an Ashkenazi family, and found them "black and inert, like leeches in a jar." For him, "The Jews sully, corrupt, rot, corrode, debase, devalue everything they touch." In Paris throughout the occupation, Giraudoux mingled socially with German officials and the higher collaborators, and a new play of his, *Sodome et Gomorrhe*, was staged there in 1943. His death early in the following year saved him from being brought to account.

Paul Claudel combined a diplomatic career and the simultaneous pursuit of literature with exceptional success. A high Catholic and a conservative politically, very much a man of the world, he seemed the contemporary standard-bearer of the values and tradition of pre-revolutionary France. Saint Louis and Joan of Arc were living symbols that he constantly invoked. Insisting that he was a poet, he cultivated an unusual flowery style even in his prose works and plays, at once rhapsodic and didactic. When W. H. Auden wrote that "time ... will pardon Paul Claudel, pardon him for writing well," he was expressing the established view of that generation that in spite of the obvious attitudinizing Claudel was a literary star of the first rank, a French Yeats or Eliot.

Claudel was born in 1868. His father and his sister, he later conceded, had been admirers of the notorious anti-Semitic polemicist Edouard Drumont, and during the Dreyfus affair he himself had not been "on the right side." His first foreign posting was in 1893, as French consul in New York. Soon afterwards he was sent for six years to China. As late as 1910, by which time Dreyfus had been rehabilitated, Claudel was writing to his fellow Catholic Péguy, a militant for the faith but contrarily a Dreyfusard, "I have difficulty understanding how you can deny the role of Jewry in this affair. I have lived in all the countries of the world and everywhere I have seen the newspapers and public opinion in the hands of the Jews. I was in Jerusalem in December 1899 and at the moment of the second condemnation [of Dreyfus] I saw the rage of those lice with a human face who live in Palestine on the razzias which their kith and kin operate against Christianity." In his diary on February 3, 1900, Jules Renard recorded a meeting with Claudel. "His soul is queasy [*son âme a mauvais estomac*]. He comes back to the horror he feels for the Jews, he can't stand the sight or smell of them." Consul in Frankfurt in 1910, Claudel wrote in his diary, "Here I am representing the French Republic in this capital of international Jewry."

In the early years of the twentieth century, he first began portraying Jewish characters for literary effect. Ali Habenichts and his daughter Sichel are names he gives to a Jewish father and daughter in a trilogy of plays. Money-making, the wish to assimilate, and the absence of any patriotism are their distinguishing traits. The place of the Jew in the modern world is in question. Claudel puts into the mouth of Sichel, "But for us Jews, there's no little scrap of earth so large as a gold coin." Claudel commissioned Darius Milhaud to write musical accompaniments, and after years of collaboration he could say in a letter to him, "What a pity that you aren't a Catholic. We could do great things together."

In the Twenties, Claudel was ambassador in Tokyo and then Washington (where he received Morand). His outlook seems to have evolved when one of his sons married a woman named Christine, whose sister, Aliki, was the wife of Paul-Louis Weiller. An eminent Frenchman of Jewish origins and a convert to Christianity, Weiller had been an air force ace in the First War. He was the owner and managing director of Gnome et Rhône, a huge company and leading manufacturer of aircraft engines. By virtue of his position, Weiller moved in the highest political and military circles, and in 1935 he appointed Claudel to the board of the company, paying him a large salary. Perhaps it was fortuitous, but the following year Claudel wrote an open letter to the World Jewish Congress, with a sentence objecting to the Nuremburg race laws just passed. "The abominable and stupid legislation directed against those of your religion in Germany fills me with indignation and horror."

The demise of the Third Republic's parliamentary regime in June 1940 enthused him. After sixty years, he wrote in his diary, France had been delivered "from the yoke of the radical and anti-clerical party (professors, lawyers, Jews, freemasons)." "Education without God" was a prime cause of the present plight. The replacement of democracy by an authoritarian system based on Catholic values had long been his ideal. He knew Marshal Pétain, and many years earlier had described him in his diary as "A typical French general, as illustrated in popular novels." Pétain had voted for Claudel's election to the Academy in 1935. Nonetheless, Claudel disapproved of unqualified collaboration with Germany, as recommended by some Catholics, notably Cardinal Baudrillart. Already in his early seventies, Claudel had retired to Brangues, his country house in the non-occupied zone.

On October 6, 1940, Paul-Louis Weiller was arrested

57

on trumped-up charges to do with establishing a factory in Morocco, but evidently only because he was a prominent Jew. Next day Claudel went to Vichy to intercede for him, and then petitioned Pétain but to no effect. Soon afterwards Weiller's French citizenship was revoked, and his property confiscated. Released from prison, Weiller was able to escape to New York.

Claudel's frame of mind remains unclear, because on December 27 he published an ode to Pétain, presenting him as the national savior, an almost saintly figure in the footsteps of Saint Louis and Joan of Arc. Claudel's motive, it is often suggested, was self-interest. Vichy was to subsidize the performance of his plays, in particular *Le Soulier de satin*, put on in Paris like Giraudoux's play in 1943 and a cultural highlight of the occupation. To an interviewer after the war, Claudel explained his enthusiasm for Pétain with the sentence, "He took me in [*Il m'a eu*]."

Be that as it may, on December 24, 1941, Claudel wrote to Isaïe Schwartz, the Grand Rabbi of France, taking a position against the Statut des Juifs, and expressing "the disgust, horror and indignation which all decent Frenchmen and specially Catholics feel in respect of the injustices, the despoiling, all the ill treatment of which our Jewish compatriots are now the victims." Catholics, he concluded all in his own vein, could never forget that "Israel is always the eldest Son of the promise [i.e., of God], as it is today the eldest Son of suffering." The rank of *"Ambassadeur de France"* after his signature made this act of civil courage unique. The letter was published, and the Vichy authorities judged it "particularly brazen," while also suspecting Claudel of facilitating Weiller's flight abroad. The police duly searched Brangues and kept Claudel under observation. In keeping with the twists and turns of that tormented period, Claudel on September 28, 1944 published in the *Figaro littéraire* an ode to de Gaulle, as embarrassing in its high-flown obsequiousness as his previous ode to Pétain.

Claudel was one of the earliest to understand that the Holocaust was an event like no other, and a stain for ever on Christian Europe. But there might be something "providential" about it, or what he also detected as a "redeeming effectiveness" (*"efficacité rédemptrice"*). For the remainder of his life he pondered in his visionary manner on "The Mystery of Israel" and its "Vocation." To support the state of Israel was in some measure to make amends; his approval of it was genuine, and marked the complete reversal of the animus against "lice with a human face" which once had possessed him. The place of the Jews in the modern world remained in question, however. For him, Jews were a people apart but also with an ecumenical mission all their own, possessors of the Holy Land not through any historic link or right but as citizens of Humanity, with "a message addressed to man as he emerged pure from the hands of his Creator." Even for someone trying as sincerely as Claudel to come to grips with the events of his times, in other words, Jews were not human beings like any other, but still creatures of other purposes, divine though these might be.

EIGHT

The Rescue of
the Mufti of Jerusalem

"WE HATE FRANCE—she is the enemy of Islam and religion because she is governed by atheists and Jews," Makki al-Nasiri, one Arab nationalist propagandist among many with a similar view, had declared on Mussolini's Radio Rome in 1938. At that same time, a tract distributed throughout North Africa had the words: "The Jew feeds on you like vermin feeds on sheep; France protects him; he is the agent of France, the tool of France. Germany is arresting and persecuting Jews and confiscating their possessions. If you weren't the slaves of France, you could do the same." Collapse in 1940, and subsequent German occupation, exhausted France's moral and political authority as an imperial power. As leader of the Free French, General de Gaulle on a flying visit to Brazzaville in January 1944 had made a speech promising independence to French colonies and mandates in the Middle East, a promise which evidently he had no intention of meeting any time soon. Arab nationalists, however, in North Africa and the Levant now saw themselves invited to rebel and seize power.

On May 8, 1945, the very day marking Allied victory in Europe, Algerians rioted in the provincial town of Setif. More than one hundred French people were killed, and as many injured. According to best estimates, at least 6,000 Algerians died in the reprisals that followed. At the same time, law and order broke down in Syria and Lebanon. More than four hundred Syrians were killed, and the parliament in Damascus was destroyed. British forces temporarily in Syria and Lebanon as a result of the war ordered the much weaker French units back to barracks, in effect negating French rule and handing independence to both countries. Britain's Minister Plenipotentiary there was General Sir Edward Spears, "not far short of a viceroy," according to his biographer Max Egremont. In the Paris Assembly, the French foreign minister Georges Bidault warned the British, "*Hodie mihi, cras tibi*"—today me, tomorrow you. In French eyes, the long-drawn British policy of using their position in Palestine and Egypt to undermine France was coming to a head.

That same May, Haj Amin al-Husseini, the Mufti of Jerusalem, his staff of some sixteen lieutenants, and Gunther Obenhoff, the officer assigned to him by the Gestapo, left what had been German-occupied Silesia and fled to Switzerland. Denied asylum there, they found themselves in the hands of the French authorities. Haj Amin had been responsible for the rejection of any idea of partitioning Palestine, and for precipitating the Arab revolt of 1936 in which many British personnel as well as Jews and considerably more Arabs had been killed. With French connivance, he had escaped in 1938 to Lebanon, going on to participate in the 1941 anti-British and pro-Nazi coup in Iraq, and finally fleeing to Berlin.

Photographs show him in his clerical robes and turban in the company of Hitler, Goebbels, Himmler, and Eichmann, either in private meetings or at public occasions, including a tour of Auschwitz intended to promote the Holocaust. A particular contribution was to be his enthusiastic campaign to recruit a Bosnian Muslim division for the S.S. After the Allies invaded North Africa in November 1942 and Germans had taken over Vichy France in November 1942, Haj Amin wrote memoranda urging Hitler to exploit the local populations in order to break "the Judeo–Anglo-Saxon stranglehold." On December 2, 1942 he wrote a letter to Shakib Arslan, another who identified Arab nationalism with Nazism. The turn of the war brought one piece of good news, Haj Amin thought, namely that "France, the great enemy of Muslims and Arabs, is broken; . . . she will never again be able to play an important role in world politics." This letter had surfaced in Berlin, and the French could be in no doubt that Haj Amin in his inner self gloated at their downfall, and that in spite of France's best efforts to woo them the huge majority of Arabs shared this outlook. In the light of his record, the Americans, the British, and the Yugoslavs wanted him extradited as a war criminal.

On May 11, 1943, the Ministry of the Interior briefed the Quai d'Orsay that a qualified Gestapo official under interrogation had described Haj Amin as "the brains of German espionage in all Muslim countries." Next day Lescuyer in the embassy in Cairo sent a telegram confirming what was to become policy (M.A.E./Afrique-Levant/1944–1965/Généralités/Vol. 30). According to this telegram, Haj Amin held the future of Palestine in his hands and as a religious leader could impose his will on the Arab League, then newly formed. "Measures of coercion taken in respect of the Mufti might prejudice our cause in Muslim countries. The Mufti has certainly betrayed the Allied cause. But he has above all betrayed Britain without affecting us directly. Seemingly, therefore, nothing obliges us to undertake any action in his regard which could only harm us in the Arab countries." A telegram from the Beirut embassy on May 16 asked for clarification of Haj Amin's status, in order "with all necessary discretion to reassure his friends," and to remit to him money offered by Sami Solh, a former Lebanese prime minister. Chauvel, now director general of the Quai d'Orsay, in a note marked "Urgent" on May 18 confirmed to the Minister of War what French diplomats in the field were telling him, that Haj Amin was "capable of imposing himself on the Muslim community" and in particular the Arab countries, "factors to be borne in mind since the problem of Palestine remains open."

By May 23, Chauvel had made up his mind, informing relevant embassies, "In spite of the very heavy accusations weighing against him, Haj Amin is to be treated with consideration." The reason given for this was his "religious prestige." An unsigned note of May 30 (M.A.E./

Afrique-Levant/1944–1965/Généralités/Vol. 30) is apparently in Chauvel's handwriting. He asserts, "The Quai d'Orsay's ignorance of Muslim problems has always been remarkable," implying that his powers of analysis are far superior. France should have kept Haj Amin safe before the war rather than expelling him from Syria. Discouragement alone had led Haj Amin to Hitler. "At the moment when the policy of General Spears is tending to throw us completely out of Syria, we must make use of the strong personality who has fallen into our hands and above all refuse to deliver him to our English friends."

Haj Amin was housed in a villa in the Paris suburbs. With him were two secretaries and a cook supplied by the Paris mosque. Captain Deveaux (spelt Devaux and even Desvaux in some documents), a *Police judiciaire* officer, had responsibility for security and surveillance. The Quai d'Orsay's go-between, Henri Ponsot, a former High Commissioner and Ambassador in Lebanon and Syria, was impressed by Haj Amin's "certain air of dignity and aristocratic grace," as well as by his intellectual mastery and correct French. As for war crimes, Haj Amin claimed that he knew nothing about extermination camps and had never heard of Karl Hichman, in Ponsot's (perhaps deliberately) garbled version of Adolf Eichmann. Approvingly, Ponsot passed on Haj Amin's view that France and the Arab states could easily come to an accord to settle the future of both Syria and Palestine as they wished. Britain was unable "to break loose from the influence that the Jewish world exercised on its politics." What

Haj Amin offered, Ponsot reported on June 26, was either a "positive" collaboration, in which case he would calm the general Arab agitation concerning Syria, or a "negative" collaboration, in which case he would provoke crises in Palestine, Egypt, Iraq and Transjordan, "to the benefit of our own policy" (these words of Ponsot's are lightly scratched out on the document, M.A.E./Afrique–Levant/1944–1965/Généralités/Vol. 30/K14.18).

At the end of July, Haj Amin was moved into a comfortable country house in Bougival, where he could receive visitors, walk in the park under supervision and visit Paris, where Lanvin the couturier cut him a civilian suit. The documents hint at financial and material help in conditions of growing good will. Louis Massignon was France's most distinguished orientalist. Reporting on August 14 to the Quai d'Orsay on his visit to Haj Amin, he could not resist saying that they had spoken Arabic and he had addressed the Mufti as *"za'imnaa"* or Our Leader. Haj Amin "is persuaded that he can launch a durable Franco-Arab cooperation," in the belief that "France had to have a pro-Islamic policy" and he asked for permission to meet Arab diplomats as "time was pressing, if the Zionists attack" (M.A.E./Afrique–Levant/1944–1965/Généralités/Vol. 30/K14.18/000085).

The talk in the Quai d'Orsay was already of letting Haj Amin go free. From the London embassy, René Massigli on August 17 warned that sending Haj Amin to an Arab country might assuage Muslims but if thanks to France he were to install himself anywhere near Transjordan and Palestine, "he will start his intrigues again." Should the

Betrayal

British insist on having Haj Amin brought to trial, Chauvel commented in October, "we should probably be obliged to have the party slip directly into Switzerland." In April 1946, the French press published an officially inspired announcement that the government would not prevent Haj Amin's departure to an Arab country. Taking the hint, Haj Amin on May 29, 1946 left Orly airport on a TWA flight to Cairo. Under the name of a retainer who had been with him in Nazi Germany, and wearing his new Lanvin suit, he traveled on a false Syrian passport. In Cairo members of the French Legation had regular interviews with Haj Amin. The Minister, Gilbert Arvengas, praised Haj Amin's "quite particular interest in French cultural activity," but he had the sense to express reservations about Haj Amin's trustworthiness.

Haj Amin himself on October 11 made an official declaration of thanks to the French government, for the hospitality and the tacit approval of his escape. But Captain Deveaux had been suspended on grounds of negligence, and Haj Amin pleaded for him. Deveaux, he wrote, was "for me a friend endowed with exceptional qualities. To my mind he is a great diplomat and it would be regrettable if France were deprived of his services." He need not have worried. Deveaux had already been reinstated, and not long afterwards would be promoted. All had connived in a charade. In a secret annex to his declaration of thanks, Haj Amin harped on a favorite theme: the British and American governments were in the hands of the Jews. "It had been the same in Germany, where, thanks to the natural simplicity of the leaders, the Jews prior to Hitler had taken hold of all the commanding reins." Now, he told the French, "your civilization, your spirituality, your liberalism" would bring them and the Arabs together.

From Cairo, Haj Amin went to Lebanon. There he remained in touch with French officials for purposes of intrigue. On June 29, 1949, for instance, Gilbert Arvengas was reporting from the Cairo embassy (M.A.E./Vol. 224/RL/MA) how a colleague by the name of Lescot had visited the Mufti, to listen to him praising the dynamism of King Farouk of Egypt, in reality soon to be overthrown. He was also enthusiastic about Husni Zaim, who had seized power in Syria and, in reality again, was about to be murdered in another coup. To the Mufti's satisfaction, France had provided Husni Zaim with arms, and he reassured Lescot of "a prompt restoration of the traditional Franco-Islamic friendship." From France, he hoped for a more active attitude over Palestine. He was emphatic about provoking a general uprising against King Abdullah of Jordan, and indeed soon arranged to have him shot dead in Jerusalem. As best he could, he was orchestrating his "negative" policy of violence against the emerging state of Israel, a policy which could only deepen the ruin of the Palestinians and which has bedeviled the Middle East ever since.

NINE

The Mystique of Louis Massignon

Louis Massignon revitalized for his contemporaries the assumptions that France was a Muslim power and that Jews had to fit into other peoples' conception of them, without right to any identity they might forge for themselves. France's pre-eminent orientalist in his day, and a professor at the Collège de France from 1925 onwards, he nonetheless utilized scholarship to promote personal and political prejudices. As Elie Kedourie pointed out in an essay "Politics and the Academy," Massignon's wild abandon made him a prime example of the *trahison des clercs* which Julien Benda in his book of that title held to be degrading public discourse, and was nothing less than treason to the very concept of an intellectual. A particularly brilliant misfit, he was a fabulator with a personality strong enough to persuade those who listened to him that the quirks of his imagination corresponded to the real world. Accordingly he was to spread mystification right through the Quai d'Orsay to lasting effect.

The Mystique of Louis Massignon

Born in 1883, Massignon was the son of an artist and sculptor, and brought up in the milieu of the Symbolists for whom decadence was all the rage. As a young man on a visit to Morocco, he met Marshal Lyautey, who believed that the country offered every opportunity for the expansion of French imperialism. In Cairo and Baghdad before the First World War, he learnt the languages of the Middle East, and did the initial research that led to professorship and his reputation. It pleased him to adopt the robes and turban of a student at Al-Azhar, the historic center of Muslim devotion in Cairo. A genuine scholar, his special study concerned Mansur al-Hallaj, a medieval Shia mystic tortured to death on a gibbet as a heretic in Baghdad in 922, and impossibly visualized by him as a Muslim Christ figure. A Spanish friend, Luis de Cuadra, introduced him to the homosexual debauchery of Cairo. Soon afterwards, consumed by remorse, he had a religious epiphany, a vision of what he called "the Divine Fire." De Cuadra, a convert to Islam, committed suicide a few years later in a Spanish prison. The unhappy fate of his friend was to mark Massignon for the rest of his life, as Robert Irwin judges in *For Lust of Knowing*, his comprehensive account of Orientalists and their work. The complex interaction of sin and redemption, in Massignon's conviction, gave all human behaviour its value.

One friend was Charles de Foucauld, founder of the missionary order of the White Fathers, later murdered in his Saharan retreat by Ottoman soldiers. Massignon believed that he too had some such religious vocation, with an accompanying posture of martyrdom as suffered by both Christ and Mansur al-Hallaj. But marriage was part and parcel of the high Catholic sacrament, although something which hardly interfered with his incessant travels and his work. Paul Claudel, another long-standing friend, was one of the witnesses at Massignon's wedding. From his posting in Prague, Claudel on February 8, 1911 wrote to him: "You would make an incomparable agent. I have dropped the word to my friend Berthelot to whom I must introduce you one day." The Ottoman authorities in Mesopotamia had indeed arrested him as a spy. Although the Massignon files in the Quai d'Orsay remain closed, enough is in the public domain to show that he was some sort of roving ambassador engaged in secret and confidential work. Loosely described as head of a "Scientific Mission," he traveled on a diplomatic passport. Algeria, Morocco and Syria were among his special concerns, and in one of his books he admitted, "I was aware I was sailing under false colors in Damascus from 1920 to 1945."

In 1917, as a member of the Georges-Picot mission, he was present when the British captured and entered Jerusalem. Lawrence of Arabia was also there; they spoke together in Arabic, and Massignon found fault with Lawrence's crude dialect. They were two of a kind. And just as Lawrence always suspected the worst of the French, so Massignon always suspected the worst of the British.

For Massignon as for Claudel, Jews were a "Mystery," whose purpose was to conduct their private dialogue with God to the ultimate benefit of Christianity. He took some time making up his mind how Zionism fitted into this classic Catholic scheme of things. After meeting Chaim Weizmann, he referred to him as the "Nasi," or prophet in Hebrew—he enjoyed blinding the Quai d'Orsay with his science. Work on the land might be redemptive for a few proletarian Jews, but in the background, he warned as early as 1920, was "the horrible Israel of cosmopolitans, bankers with no country of their own who have exploited anglo-saxon imperialism (Sassoon, Sir Herbert Samuel, Lord Reading, Lord Rothschild, Schiff, etc), eating you down to the bone." In the Middle East he sometimes took to wearing a Franciscan habit, as much a disguise as Arab robes and a turban had been. Visiting Jerusalem and Tel Aviv in 1934 he detected "powerful financial interventions" which alone enabled Zionism to survive. The conviction hardened that only "a Franco-Islamic bloc" could save the Holy Land, indeed the whole Middle East.

Nazareth to him had unique sacramental significance for its association with the Virgin Mary. Fighting in the town during the Arab revolt of 1936 was sacrilege. Jews had to learn Arabic and become Palestinian, otherwise they were "disloyal," a key concept for him; they were betraying Arab hospitality. In an article in 1939 he deplored how instead of Sephardi Jews speaking Arabic, "Germanized Ashkenazim have taken the Palestinian issue into their hands, with the perfect and implacable technique of the most exasperating of colonialisms: slowly pushing the Arab 'natives' towards the desert." Simultaneously he deplored the number of Jews fleeing into France to escape Nazi persecution, and argued that

French Jews were leading the country to destruction. At the outbreak of war, he served under Giraudoux in charge of propaganda to Muslim countries. His self-dramatizing cast of mind is revealed by a remark he made at the time to Vincent Mansour Monteil, a devoted pupil and himself a convert to Islam: "My country is the Arab world." In that same spirit he had once written about God to Claudel, "It is in Arabic no doubt that He is pleased that I should one day serve Him." Out of mortification, he fasted during Ramadan. As Robert Irwin put it with exactly weighed observations, Massignon was "an unsystematic racist," and his identification with Arab and Muslim culture arose at least in part because "he did not like Jews very much."

After the war, Massignon campaigned with passionate fury against the creation of the state of Israel. Any agreement with the Zionists was wrong, and besides, "would convulse our North Africa." The Jewish national home was "an imposture in which we should not be accomplices." Not really a nation, Israel had to be either something more or something less. Israel "signifies nothing unless it lives through spirituality, and if this spirituality is exclusive, as it is trying to ensure against the Muslim Arabs, it will be a catastrophe." He founded a "Comité chrétien d'Entente France-Islam," enrolling diplomats to help him lobby for the cause. First and foremost, the Holy Places had to remain in French Catholic hands, and he too based the argument for this on the architecture of churches such as the Holy Sepulchre or Saint Anne's in Jerusalem. Any Italian claim, as proposed by the Vatican, was merely incidental. In an extended polemic in print, he maintained that the notorious "blood libel" accusing the Jews of needing Christian blood for their rites had an authentic historical basis.

The United Nations vote in November 1947 in favor of partition—and the Quai d'Orsay's concurrence in that vote—appalled him. The language of his frequent articles in Catholic publications such as *Témoignage Chrétien* and *L'Aube* became infused with religiosity and political hysteria to the point of incoherence. Christian and Muslim recognition of Israel had "no value *de jure*." "The State without a Messiah of Israel" had been formed at the expense of the Arabs, who were "victims of repulsive Yankee technology." Israel, he was to tell Martin Buber in what even by his standards was a far-fetched accusation, had to stop working to exploit oil on behalf of "Atlantic speculators." Obsessed more than ever by Nazareth and the Virgin Mary, he insisted, "The world will never have a just peace until Israel reconsiders its rejection [*revisera le procès*] of the Mother of Jesus." Visiting Israel in February 1949, he felt his "heart pierced by the ignominy of the Jews." Jews were evidently sinners beyond all hope of redemption. An angry Claudel broke off a lifetime's friendship, and noted in his diary that Massignon "has gone off the rails as usual."

In 1950 in Cairo, the city where he had discovered his homosexuality, Massignon took holy orders as a priest in the eastern Melkite church. In a final somersault, he militated for the independence of French North Africa, thus undercutting French claims to be a Muslim power.

Right up to his death in 1963, his sense of guilt and sin meshed with the innate conviction of intellectual superiority and his intimation of "Divine fire." Many a Quai d'Orsay colleague was to assert afterwards that to meet Massignon was to be in the presence of genius. Massignon's learning and his showmanship served to reinforce the Quai d'Orsay then and since in its collective view that France and the world of Islam shared a common destiny; and also that it could define Jews—and ordain their future—better than Jews were able to do for themselves.

TEN

"A Pernicious Example and a Great Peril"

NOMINALLY A VICTOR in the Second World War, the France of the Fourth Republic was in reality more like one of the defeated. Its standing in the world had to be rebuilt virtually from scratch. In 1945 somewhere between one and two hundred soldiers or members of the Resistance were given the reward of admission without an examination to the "career" at the Quai d'Orsay. That year too, the École Nationale d'Administration was created for the purpose of training civil servants, and every year afterwards a handful of its graduates became diplomats. In theory, here was a new dispensation. In practice, the institutional mind-set of the Quai d'Orsay survived intact. In the office concerned with Jewish affairs that he had occupied within the Quai d'Orsay since the late 1920s, Louis Canet on December 3, 1945 could once more warn his superiors as though the recent war had not occurred to act "with a great deal of prudence and circumspection" concerning recognition of a Jewish youth association on the grounds that "it is of interest to international Jewry, Freemasonry and international working-class organizations" (M.A.E.-C.P.C./Afrique–Levant/Généralités/Vol. 23/1944–1965/K 13 16).

As far as the Middle East was concerned, Zionism was more of a danger than ever to what French diplomats believed would otherwise have been a smooth and advantageous relationship with Arab countries. Numerous commentaries and testimonies underline the persistence of this attitude. The historian Jean-Baptiste Duroselle mildly observes that the first post-war foreign minister Bidault was "not unreceptive to the arguments of the Islamists in the Quai d'Orsay." Christian Pineau, a subsequent foreign minister well disposed towards Israel, happened to be the son-in-law of Jean Giraudoux. In his autobiography he writes that the Quai d'Orsay was motivated in its Middle East policy by a "more or less conscious" anti-Semitism. The secretary general, Jean Chauvel, would brief journalists against Pineau and frustrate his initiatives. In his own memoirs, Chauvel himself makes the revealingly slanted remark that at the end of the war, "Jews and Communists, formerly untouchables and moreover deported or living underground, had been reintegrated with honor into the community."

The archives expose the limitations of the Quai d'Orsay. In April 1945, a committee was set up "to examine the different problems posed by the Jewish question." The committee's name, Comité d'Etude des Questions Juives, its purposes and the language it deployed, seem a hang-over from Vichy. Its president, Henri Ponsot, considered one of the department's most eminent authorities on the Middle East, was at the same time regularly calling on the Mufti, Haj Amin, to exonerate and promote him. In his version of the usual grandiloquent rhetoric, he underlined that France as "a Muslim empire" had to be attentive to Arab demands.

Entre Paris et Jerusalem, by Tsilla Hershco, is a definitive archive-based study of the French position in the crucial years leading to the creation of Israel. In close detail she demonstrates how French policy was "frequently inspired by the desire to please the Arabs" while also displaying the Quai d'Orsay's traditional hostility to Zionism as a danger to French interests, and in particular to the holy sites the French claimed to be protecting. She turns a spotlight on an anonymous official from the Quai d'Orsay who presented a preparatory document in the genuine Vichy mode. This threw the blame for wartime persecution of Jews in France wholly on to the Germans, and went on to recommend a reasonable restitution for injustices done, but only subject to "suitable precautions to prevent the recapturing by Jews of influential posts in which their massive presence would no longer be easily accepted by a public opinion that is now awakened." The Zionist movement could in any case not absorb hundreds of thousands of Jews without causing serious problems to the Arab world. The Committee was therefore to study the prospects for a Jewish state somewhere in central or eastern Europe. This, the anonymous author maintained, was a "humanitarian" solution that would "liberate the peoples from an obsession which has literally, in these last years, poisoned Europe."

A report of the committee's meeting on April 21, 1945 states that the internationalization of the British Mandate in Palestine appears imminent, and France may therefore have a new part to play in the region. "It is probable that many Israelites who were obliged under one pressure or another to leave their country of origin or their residence, would not like to return there. One can ask if on the one hand it might be useful to include in the peace treaties minority clauses in favor of Israelites, and if on the other hand, it will be desirable to favor, by some means or other, their establishment either in Palestine or another territory to be decided." The Holocaust and its consequences feature in the archives of the Quai d'Orsay only in this contorted and euphemistic style. In any case, the committee rapidly concluded that Zionism faced "insurmountable obstacles" and Palestine was not the right place for a Jewish state. Jerusalem "could not be placed under the exclusive authority of a political power unable to share."

Zionists with whom French diplomats had dealings are blackguarded in various documents. Ben-Gurion is said to be "avid with ambition." At the top right-hand corner of a personal dossier devoted to him are the handwritten words, "Nationality; Jewish" (M.A.E.-C.P.C./Levant/Palestine/1944–1965/Vol. 424.). Also under that reference, the dossier of Moshe Shertok (afterwards Sharett) carries the same characterization, and a separate note says of him, "Like all his compatriots he is highly gifted as a journalist of propaganda, but much less as a politician." Abba Eban "possesses the art of playing offended and making a travesty of facts." The Haifa consul, Pierre Landy, met Menachem Begin and wrote, "Of modest demeanor, he has the humble exterior of a small-time shop-keeper [*le dehors effacé d'un petit négociant*]." Walter Eytan was director general of the Israeli foreign ministry. He, it was reported, was "completely impervious to the conceptions of the Latin world. . . . He benefits from the prejudice in favor of all Jews educated in England or Germany, who here cut figures of great culture compared to the mass of politicians or functionaries originally from eastern Europe." Max Fischer was the Jewish Agency representative in Paris, and later first Israeli ambassador there. After a meeting in Haifa, consul Pierre Landy reported that Fischer had contrasted support in French public opinion and the press for the Jewish state with the "disagreeable stance" of the Quai d'Orsay. Fischer's generalization was true enough. Landy's own outlook was revealed in one of his despatches by his use of the phrase "the Israeli Gestapo." For him, the towns of Acre and Nazareth were "nothing but two concentration camps, for the Arabs and even for foreigners."

French representatives in Cairo and Beirut, Damascus and Amman, insisted more and more urgently that any support for Zionism and the nascent state of Israel was bound to aggravate Arab nationalism and therefore harm French interests. Moral issues, right and wrong, were not involved; power was at stake, exclusive of everything else. Armand du Chayla, Minister in Lebanon, was to compare Israel to the wartime Japanese on account of "an equally exacerbated will to power" and which would lead to a comparable catastrophe. Others in the department tried to build more positively on France's cultural presence and defense of Christianity in the Holy Land. The territory of the British Mandate at its close included some seventy French institutions, of which thirty-six were schools with 8,000 pupils between them. The majority of French cultural and scholarly centers, hospitals, and charities, were in Jerusalem, and all were Catholic. (The Alliance Israélite schools taught in French, and were for Jewish children, though open to other denominations). The French contribution was real enough, but in presenting the case that they deserved privilege and supremacy, French diplomats were arguing from chauvinism and sentimentality rather than from hard facts on the ground. Afrique-Levant, the ministry's department specializing in the issue, demonstrated what Tsilla Hershco sums up as, "a good dose of incomprehension of the region's prevalent political reality."

France took whatever diplomatic measures were available in the United Nations and behind the scenes to avert and to delay the crucial vote of November 29, 1947 to partition Mandatory Palestine. Its delegate to the UN, Alexandre Parodi, was later to explain that France had prevaricated out of a wish to maintain good relations with the Arab world. An anonymous official of the Quai d'Orsay wrote on December 1 to the Foreign Minister to regret that France's vote finally in favor of partition had wrecked long-term efforts to improve the French image in Arab eyes, and that France was now a "banana republic," unable to hold its own against Britain which had abstained in the vote. In a diary entry on June 29, 1948, the pro-Israel Vincent Auriol, then President of the Republic, recorded the depths of mystification and paradox to which French policy had sunk. Calling on Auriol, Parodi had maintained that a Jewish state in the midst of the Arab world was a guarantee of stability, and so in French interest; the Jewish state therefore had to be protected, but cautiously enough to avoid anything like an Arab defeat.

The Quai d'Orsay continued to think of Jews as people unable to take their fate into their own hands, failing completely to comprehend the Zionist response to Nazi persecution. Consul general in Jerusalem, Comte Guy du Chaylard (and not to be confused with du Chayla in Beirut), for instance, doubted that Jews had the capacity to found a state. On May 17, 1945, he reported to the director of the Afrique-Levant department that persecution had not extinguished in Jews the memories of their countries of origin and their "Germanic Kultur," in his phrase: "I am fully convinced that the greatest number of these refugees will leave Palestine where many of them are sojourning only for the sake of security, as soon as circumstances allow." Returning to this theme on September 3, 1945, he spoke of recent immigrants indulging "in a sort of free tourism." The stereotype of Jewish cowardice clashed with the stereotype of Jews as Nazis, but it penetrated the Quai d'Orsay quite as deeply. Jacques Dumaine, an ambassador, published a diary with the title *Quai d'Orsay 1945–1951* and under the date September 8, 1950 he noted down a reflection that came to him while on a walk in Paris, that panic is "one of the original nervous reactions of the Jewish race." He drew the conclusion, "even before practicing business, the Jews felt the need to flee."

René Neuville was consul general in Jerusalem from 1946 to 1952. As an archeologist, he had had experience of Mandatory Palestine and its troubles between the wars. Undoubtedly intelligent and assiduous, he was as sincere as he was narrow-minded. His inability to come to terms with the idea of a Jewish state offers a case study in the formation of policy within the Quai d'Orsay. Jews, he wrote in a lengthy despatch on April 12, 1947, were "racist through and through ... quite as much so as their German persecutors and in spite of their democratic pretensions." From biblical times, their legislators had always striven to inculcate the sense of being the Chosen People, and this bred a xenophobia and fanaticism that should not be ascribed to mere chauvinism. The Zionist press, he further adduced, "displays beyond all possible doubt the ancestral traits of a completely Oriental cast of mind [*un génie tout oriental*]" (M.A.E.-C.P. C./Levant/ Palestine/1944–1965/Vol. 373).

For Neuville, Jews were on no account to be allowed any control over Holy Places. In the despatch of April 12, 1947, he asked what would become of French interests and institutions within a Jewish state, comprising as they did "our grandeur in the Levant." He therefore favored as much international regime as possible to protect these interests, and he opposed partition with the fanaticism that he was attributing to the Jews. Dov Yossef, the Israeli liaison officer with UN staff in Jerusalem, and in close contact with the consuls, found Neuville a fervent Catholic with a mission to make France the protector of the faith: "He saw himself designated by Providence to save the Holy City for the benefit of the Holy Church."

In another characteristic report, on April 4, 1948 (M.A.E./Vol. 211–212), Neuville warned that the dream of a Jewish state entailed the death of any hopes placed in the UN. "Here, however one hides it and whatever the higher reasons, is a victory of the past over the present, of obscurantism over enlightenment. For us French— I find cover in the more authoritative opinion of our representatives in Egypt, Syria and Amman—it is a pernicious example and a great peril." Also that month, Neuville was prophesying an Arab victory, and in true Quai d'Orsay style believed that this would lead to dangerous Arab militancy in French North Africa. Come September, Neuville was exclaiming with alarm that Herzl's vision was confounded by reality. "Israel, democratic abroad, is at home the most racist and the most totalitarian of governments."

That same month, his colleague in Tel Aviv, Jacques Charreyron, was writing that a strong and well-placed minority in the future state, "will find its prosperity in the old traditional Jewish path of international trade, which cannot be realized without the help of the brothers of the race who remain implanted outside the Promised Land." Sooner or later, he thought, "the old commercial spirit of the Jews must reclaim its rights." Meanwhile Israel was a "stain" ("*tache*") on the Arab world, though contradictorily he also concluded that it already saw itself "as master of this part of the world."

France was bound ultimately to follow the example of the great powers and recognize Israel as a fact of international life, and it did so *de facto* with bad grace in January 1949, with *de jure* recognition following four months later. Israel had already accepted restitution of all French institutions, with indemnities for any damage in the 1948 fighting, and French insistence on this as a quid pro quo of recognition was close to blackmail. Tying recognition of Israel to French rights in the country was, in Tsilla Hershco's judgment, the Quai d'Orsay's "unique initiative," and the sum total of its achievement. France further campaigned hard for the internationalization of Jerusalem. The UN decreed in 1949 that the city was a *corpus separatum*, but this remained a dead letter, with Israel and Jordan in possession of their respective halves.

Once Israel had been recognized, Edouard-Felix Guyon was appointed Minister there. He lost no time supporting the alarmist views of his consuls, informing Foreign Minister Robert Schuman on August 31, 1949, "The manner in which Israeli leaders have proceeded recalls Hitler's Reich, when after the occupation of the Baltic countries by Soviet troops in 1940, it repatriated Baltic Germans ... the Israeli leaders have acted no differently, though admittedly with less method and scientific rigor."

The Israeli foreign ministry requested that Neuville

be replaced, and at the end of 1949 he was for a while absent. Vice-consul Deciry, his stand-in, however, appeared to Israeli officials as "a patented anti-Israeli." Returning to his post in the new year, in April Neuville escorted his superior Jean Binoche, assistant director of the Afrique-Levant department, on a week's visit round Israel. The two were dismayed by the dilapidation of the French institutions. True to form, Binoche could speak of "the Romanesque French style, so noble and so pure, adopted in the twelfth century by the Crusades." As for the Arabs of the Galilee, they were living in "a vast concentration camp ... the fate reserved to the Arabs is not human." In a note to the Quai d'Orsay, he commented on his colleague Neuville. "No doubt he does not have a good character, he is susceptible, stormy, bitter, but he has an ardor which I cannot find much exemplified in the people of our house. By his own admission he hasn't succeeded in obtaining very much: but the history of the French consulates in Jerusalem is hardly more than a series of set-backs." Binoche recommended keeping Neuville in place, with the proposal to bring him to confer in Paris, along with Guyon from Tel Aviv and Dumarçay from Amman. "Today," according to the wistful Binoche, "it is indispensable for the Department to define clearly the French political line." Throwing his hand in, so to speak, Binoche suggested in a report on October 24, 1952 that "there might be advantage in instigating a special committee ... of French and Muslim personalities" to raise funds for restoration work on the Dome of the Rock, the venerable Muslim shrine in Jerusalem.

85

The crisis of independence had passed, and Israel became a functioning state, but French officials on the spot proved unable or unwilling to adjust. In a document dated May 4, 1960, for instance, Jean Binaud, the consul in Haifa, reported on a meeting of the Socialist International in that city, and the first to be held outside Europe. "To flatter the *amour-propre* of Israel," in Binaud's judgment, the delegates were "abnormally important." As for the Israelis, he sneered, they did not pass up the chance to rub in "the position as advanced post of Western civilization that they love to attribute to themselves, and the role that falls to them in the concert of nations recently obtaining independence." No less typically, C. de Sainte-Marie, the consul general in Jerusalem, on October 31, 1961 wrote an account of the visit there of Paul Minot, President of the Paris Municipal Council. At a lunch in his honour at the King David Hotel, Minot expressed to the Mayor of Jerusalem his warmest wishes "for your beautiful capital." France has always been more vociferous than other nations in refusing the status of capital to Jerusalem. No doubt Minot had been carried away by the wish to please his host, Sainte-Marie concluded primly and properly to his superiors, but visiting personalities should be warned against making "any declaration liable to harm the French position concerning the Holy City."

ELEVEN

Taking Advantage

THE COUP MOUNTED in Cairo in 1952 by Gamal Abdul Nasser and other so-called Free Officers widened Arab nationalism and Pan-Islamism into popular causes mobilizing the masses. In one Arab country after another, and throughout French North Africa especially, nationalist claimants to power soon imitated Nasser. In November 1954 a series of violent terrorist acts signalled that the Algerian National Liberation Front—FLN in its French acronym—had begun to fight for independence. Nasser's radio station, The Voice of the Arabs, regularly incited the FLN; its leaders had headquarters in Cairo, and Nasser supplied them clandestinely with arms. Lasting for eight bloody years, the conflict brought about the return of General de Gaulle to power in conditions close to civil war in France. Few lamented the end of the hapless Fourth Republic.

The Cold War between the United States and the Soviet Union was then the governing factor of international politics. In terms of culture, politics, and history, France was naturally expected to side with the United States, otherwise the West. In General de Gaulle's conception, however, France's destiny was to lead rather than to follow as some secondary ally. Throughout his political career, he had been accustomed to reclaiming strength from a position of weakness. He therefore expected that opposition to the United States would have nuisance value at worst and provide leverage at best, thus advancing the national interest in ways that consent and solidarity could not. The risk was that France's anti-Americanism might involuntarily end up doing the work of the Soviet Union or alternatively provoke the United States to take unilateral action in its own interest, which might involve ignoring French susceptibilities altogether. Unable or willing to consider the recklessness of his position, de Gaulle had confidence that he could draw the fine line that was required, and thereby make up for France's lost ground as a great power. He, his coterie of associates, and his successors were accordingly to implement decisions taken out of emotional considerations of prestige and the projection of power rather than rationality, never mind morality. The long-term effect was that France proved almost as harmful to peace and stability in the Middle East as the Soviet Union.

As a prime target of Nasser and Arab nationalism, Israel unexpectedly acquired a community of interest with France in its struggle to keep its North African empire out of the hands of Arab nationalists. Not a simple case of my enemy's enemy is my friend, this was merely an interpretation by some decision-makers of the balance of forces, and therefore open to opposition from other decision-makers. The French Ministry of Defense and the leaders of the armed forces collaborated unconditionally with Israel in the belief that this strategy would overthrow Nasser and preserve French Algeria. In spite of a few persistently hostile Catholic publications and critics such as Philippe de Saint-Robert or the journalist Jean Pleyber, the media were supportive, and so was the population at large. Guilt for war-time deportations was one element, but admiration for Israel's spirit of self-determination was widespread and genuine. More than a reversal of alliances in the style of cynical old-world diplomacy, here was open repudiation of the Quai d'Orsay and its ingrained pro-Arab policy.

Arms sales alone gave France any importance in the Middle East. In the Israeli view, the procurement of aircraft, tanks, and heavy artillery was urgent, to prevent Nasser from exploiting the military superiority given him by the Soviet Union. The United States and Britain took cover behind a declaration not to supply armaments to belligerents in the region. French manufacturers and the Ministry of Defense were eager to supply Israel. Co-signatories to the same declaration, the Quai d'Orsay ingeniously blocked sales outright, or ensured that deliveries were too minimal to be effective. Jews were also perceived as a pro-French element in North Africa, and Zionist efforts to encourage them to immigrate to Israel were greatly resented.

Inter-ministerial fighting at the time had something

conspiratorial about it. Pierre-Etienne Gilbert, French ambassador in Israel from 1953 to 1959, was altogether exceptional among his colleagues, the first French diplomat openly to admire Israel. Learning Hebrew, he became the trusted friend of Israeli leaders from Ben-Gurion downwards. Gilbert introduced the Israeli defense establishment to their counterparts in Paris, Maurice Bourgès-Maunoury, the Minister of Defense, and Abel Thomas, the director of his cabinet, and described by one authority, Sylvia K. Crosbie, as "a key man in the Fourth Republic." *Comment Israël fut sauvé*, or How Israel was Saved, is the title of Thomas's memoirs. He speaks of "our quarrels and our chicaneries with the Quai d'Orsay," and how in respect of policy concerning Israel, "it was agreed that the administration of the Quai would in no case be involved." His brother, a member of the Resistance, had died in a German concentration camp, but this was not the cause of pro-Jewish sentimentality. He and his colleagues, he stresses, sincerely held that Arab nationalism ought to be stopped in its tracks as a danger to all concerned. Consistently, the Quai d'Orsay reacted with anger and frustration to the Ministry of Defense. In March 1956, Pierre Maillard of the Afrique-Levant department was informing his Israeli interlocutor that French-Israeli arms deal were an aberration, and there was no basis for cooperation between the two countries.

The Czech arms deal of September 1955, and then the nationalization of the Suez Canal the following July, were defining events of Nasser's career. The French and Israeli cabinets were of one mind that only pre-emptive war could eliminate the danger Nasser now presented to them both. French Prime Minister Guy Mollet, a socialist, undertook to persuade the hesitant British to join what became the real conspiracy behind the 1956 Suez campaign. Foreign Minister Christian Pineau devotes a section of his memoirs, *1956 Suez*, to the uncomfortable experience he had at the Quai d'Orsay. Its members were highly qualified, he accepted, but they lacked discipline to such an extent that he could not trust them to carry out government policy. The director general, no less, gathered journalists to brief against his own minister, and to say that Pineau's position was so provisional that there was no need to worry about his ignorance and his mistakes. Consequently Pineau instructed Ambassador Gilbert to report to him alone, and, as the historian J. R. Tournoux has recorded, he further advised Bourgès-Maunoury and Abel Thomas at the Ministry of Defense, "Above all, not a word to the Quai d'Orsay!"

Coordination amid animosities and secrecies among those taking vital decisions did not—could not—lead to success. Fatefully, the United States intervened to oblige first the British and French to withdraw their invading forces, and then to compel Israel to evacuate Sinai and the Gaza Strip. In 1957, France agreed to build the nuclear plant at Dimona, an installation more up-to-date than anything the French themselves possessed at the time. From that peak, the Franco-Israeli relationship declined in inexorable stages.

Nasser's emergence as the political victor of the Suez campaign inflated Arab nationalism into the prime ideology of the Middle East. The FLN was evidently going to gain power, the French army to lose it as the remnant of the former empire fell away. Emerging from the country house where he had retreated since last he had been in office, in 1958 General de Gaulle once more enacted the role he had played in 1940 as national savior. The Suez campaign ushered in the Fifth Republic, and more ominously, transformed the regional Arab-Israeli dispute into one of the most intractable of international issues.

Methodically, the Quai d'Orsay began the disengagement from Israel. In deference to the Arab economic boycott of Israel, it succeeded in 1959 in cancelling a contract to assemble Renault cars under license in Haifa. The following year, Ben-Gurion met de Gaulle at the Elysée, and the Quai d'Orsay was at pains to ensure as a matter of formal diplomacy that this was not a state visit, and that the Israeli flag could not fly at Ben-Gurion's hotel. A professor of economics, Jean-Marcel Jeanneney, was chairman of a commission to determine foreign policy, and his official report was presented to de Gaulle in 1963. Writing the section on the Middle East, Jean Chauvel hoped to see the spread of French culture, in Lebanon and Iran especially. Israel in his judgment displayed "a heterogeneous character in relation to everything surrounding it," and this euphemism led to the conclusion that good Franco-Israeli relations "in no way give France any credit in Arabia." For the Arabs, cooperation with France "is not only acceptable. It is desired."

De Gaulle's Foreign Minister for the unprecedented period of ten years was Maurice Couve de Murville. At

Vichy, he had been a financial expert until his carefully timed departure to join the winning side in North Africa early in 1943. Ambassador in Cairo from 1950 to 1954, he appears from the documents to have been the French diplomat who met the embittered and frustrated Haj Amin for one last time. A critic of the Suez campaign, and an advocate of Algerian independence, he made his mark by particular opposition to the sale of French aircraft to Israel. Louis Massignon, he was to claim in an admiring obituary, had greatly influenced him. Golda Meir found him cold and unfriendly. Where Israel was concerned, he was a willing promoter of de Gaulle's *renversement des alliances*. In his memoirs, he rejoiced that alone among Western countries France took into consideration the points of view of the Arab world "and understood its feelings." The Quai d'Orsay was able at last to take revenge for the preceding Pineau years, and, as two Arab historians Samir Kassir and Farouk Mardam-Bey put it, successfully reaffirmed its old "Muslim policy."

The constitution of the Fifth Republic handed the conduct of foreign policy to the President with the result that the Quai d'Orsay's role was largely reduced to advice and administration. De Gaulle often elided France and the personal pronoun, as if he really were the embodiment of national grandeur that he projected himself to be. The Socialist Prime Minister Guy Mollet once commented that, "De Gaulle believes himself invested with a mission, everything has to submit to that. It's like Joan of Arc." A friend and colleague of de Gaulle's since 1942, former Foreign Minister Pineau is one among many to stress that de Gaulle's reactions were grounded in his personality rather than in objective realities. Always idiosyncratic, his words and deeds have been exhaustively explored. Commentators point out that Charles Maurras, a passionate enemy of Jews in general and in particular the pursuer of a vendetta against Dreyfus alive or dead, had once influenced him. Zionists from Ben-Gurion downwards, however, provide personal testimony of his admiration for Israel and its achievements. In contrast to the Quai d'Orsay in 1948, he approved of the creation of the state of Israel, and also the incorporation into it of Galilee and the Negev, both areas not in any partition plan but captured from the Arabs. Ambassador Pierre Gilbert quotes him saying, "The Arabs are all passion, sometimes even demented [*un monde passionel, parfois même démentiel*]. What can you do with that?" In all likelihood, his most profound belief was that Jews and Arabs, like everyone else, had to serve the purposes he allotted to them.

In his memoirs de Gaulle complained that French diplomats were far from conforming to his own outlook, "hence the necessity of closely watching and keeping a grip on French negotiators." Above all, de Gaulle aspired to great power status for France, and to that end he sought to maneuver between the United States and the Soviet Union, playing one off against the other and eventually ejecting NATO from France, in the hope that this brand of militant neutrality would muster the whole Third World behind him. Pineau again is only one among many witnesses to affirm that de Gaulle felt "a mortal hate" for the British and the Americans. The United States had the international power and projection that France could envy but never match.

As the Sixties evolved, moreover, the United States increasingly came to appreciate that Israel was a democracy, sharing its moral values, and proving a dependable ally in the Cold War. In ostensibly permanent contrast, Egypt, Syria, and other Arab countries were one-party police states in the manner of the Soviet Union that was supporting them. A sense that Israel was an obstacle to French purposes increasingly fed into Gaullist anti-Americanism. The belief accordingly hardened that the small regional power was in partnership—perhaps even conspiring—with the major international power to supplant France.

Increasingly resentful and frustrated, de Gaulle suspended further aid to the Dimona nuclear plant; he played cat-and-mouse games over sales of arms and aircraft; and after signing the peace treaty with Algeria intervened to give Jacques Roux, his new ambassador in Cairo, instructions "which would permit a more liberal attitude towards Nasser." When Abba Eban, the Israeli foreign minister, at a meeting in early 1966, expressed anxiety about the relationship with France, an irritated Couve de Murville replied, "General de Gaulle doesn't have to be patting you ceaselessly on the shoulder to reassure you."

In a series of political and military miscalculations, Nasser precipitated the Six Day War of 1967. One of his measures was to close the straits of Tiran leading to the port of Eilat. Israel was not prepared to suffer an economic

blockade of the kind. In the opinion of Couve de Murville, however, Israeli shipping did not use the straits
enough to justify going to war on that account, and de
Gaulle shared this conviction. Furthermore, he saw a
chance to enhance France's standing by resolving the
crisis through the good offices of the Great Powers. In
the run-up to the outbreak of hostilities, de Gaulle had
meetings in the Elysée with Walter Eytan, the Israeli
ambassador, and with Abba Eban, the Israeli Foreign
Minister, who flew round the world's major capitals in
the vain attempt to gain support. To Eban on May 24,
de Gaulle gave the warning that Israel should not make
war—"In any event, do not be the first to open fire!" On
June 3, Claude Lebel, director of the Afrique-Levant
division of the Quai d'Orsay, informed the Israeli embassy
that all shipment of arms to the Middle East was now
suspended. This move affected Israel alone, and was in
complete contrast to the 1956 policy of unlimited assis-
tance. Next day, Walter Eytan had a chance to tell de
Gaulle that this embargo added to the pressures on Israel
and therefore made war more likely. Referring to himself,
or perhaps France, in the third person, de Gaulle's reply
was as lofty as it was non-committal: "If you are attacked,
one wouldn't let you be destroyed [*on ne vous laissera
pas détruire*]."

"I told Eban that they shouldn't shoot first," de Gaulle
was to say with anger and hurt pride a few days later,
according to the Israeli historian Michael Bar-Zohar.
"They didn't listen to me!" He is supposed to have
uttered almost exactly these words in front of Charles

Bohlen, the American ambassador. He also told British Prime Minister Harold Wilson that some day the West would thank him, as from then on France would "be the only Western power to have any influence with the Arab governments."

True to Quai d'Orsay preoccupations, Roger Seydoux, an Arabist who had served much of his career in Tunisia and Morocco, a former director general of the ministry and now France's permanent representative at the United Nations, lost no time declaring in a speech in New York that the reunification of Jerusalem as one outcome of the war was "inopportune and not founded in law." Israeli assurances of free access to the Holy Places "touched on questions of sovereignty to which we could not remain indifferent." That November, de Gaulle ranted at a press conference that the Jews were "an elite people, self-assured and domineering" with "a burning ambition for conquest." In the ensuing outrage, de Gaulle pretended that these generalizations were intended as compliments, and he even told Chief Rabbi Kaplan so. Such an excuse did not serve to cover his bad faith, for he had included a manifestly racist remark about "the flood, sometimes rising, sometimes falling, of malevolence which they [the Jews] provoke, or more exactly which they arouse in certain countries and at certain periods."

In January 1969, in response to Palestinian hijackers operating out of Lebanon, Israeli commandos blew up thirteen Lebanese civil aircraft in Beirut. Nobody was hurt in this largely symbolic action. "It's unbelievable, without any sense," de Gaulle was to complain of the Israelis. "They think they can do as they like." Malicious calculation, he believed, lay behind it. The Israelis, he told his assistant Jean d'Escrienne, had used French-made aircraft to destroy other French-made aircraft. "If they had used American equipment, they would have run the risk of reviving the hostility of the Arab world against the United States." The intention was therefore to make France the target of this hostility. The embargo was now extended to the delivery to Israel of all weapons, defensive as well as offensive. France thereby relinquished any influence it might have had on Israel.

In a polemic of great force with the title *De Gaulle and the Jews*, Raymond Aron, one of the leading political thinkers of the age, took exception to the stereotyping of Jews as self-assured and domineering, and went on to argue that de Gaulle had pushed Israel into the arms of the United States. Graver still, de Gaulle had "knowingly, voluntarily, opened a new era in Jewish and perhaps anti-Semitic history. Everything becomes possible once more, everything may start again. Granted, there is no question of persecution: only ill will. This is not a time for contempt but for suspicion." He furthermore grasped the realpolitik fact that de Gaulle's policy indeed had the effect of delivering Israel henceforward to what Gaullists liked to call "the American hegemony."

In a notorious article in *Le Monde* on February 27, 1970, (and therefore after de Gaulle's departure from office) René Massigli, highly respected as a former ambassador to London and afterwards director general of the

Quai d'Orsay, spoke for the ministry by repeating the ancient accusation that French Jews who supported Israel were guilty of double loyalties. The deliberate shifting of the climate of opinion against Israel could not fail to hurt Jews generally, as Aron had foretold.

Although de Gaulle had once been wary of the Quai d'Orsay, in common with his diplomats he ended by speaking of France as a "Muslim power." In his *Mémoires* he was to be summary: "no strategic, political or economic state of affairs will last unless it gets Arab support." His self-importance stranded his country in contradiction, prejudice, and grudge. François Mauriac, a Nobel Prize winner and fervent Gaullist, judged that policy towards Israel had played an important part in de Gaulle's downfall. Some months before the decisive referendum in 1969, Mauriac wrote, "I saw men whom the General's policy towards Jerusalem had driven mad." The Quai d'Orsay had won, but there was nothing to show for it.

TWELVE

Men and Matters

In the aftermath of the Six Day War of 1967, the Middle East replaced central Europe as the arena of the Cold War most likely to lead to unforeseen—and so perhaps uncontrollable—large-scale military clashes. The 1968 Soviet invasion of Czechoslovakia, for example, evoked criticism but not even a hint of armed retaliation on the part of NATO or the United States. In the Middle East, the United States and the Soviet Union were locked irretrievably in a struggle involving imponderables of ideology, power, and prestige, and each committed to their friends and allies. Raising the stakes was oil, which producers for the first time began to brandish as a weapon, placing an embargo on sales to countries friendly to Israel like the Netherlands, or raising the price fast enough and high enough to hold Western economies to ransom. In Washington, as in Moscow, a mistake, a misunderstanding, might magnify into a superpower collision with consequences that risked testing political skills and wisdom to the limits.

So dominating has de Gaulle and his legacy been that every subsequent French president, whether Gaullist or socialist, has tried to cleave to his view of France's pre-eminent place in the world, with marginal shadings of emphasis according to circumstances. For the sake of influence or money, France has consequently sought out one Arab dictator after another with whom to establish a mutually beneficial relationship. Wily and unscrupulous by definition, these dictators have got the best of the deal, time and again placing France in the invidious position of backing cruel and absolute one-man rule. Whether conservative or socialist nominally, the politicians responsible appear similar in character, standardized so to speak, no more distinguishable in their address to the questions of the Middle East than the professional advisors upon whom they had to rely.

President from 1969 until his sudden death in 1974, Georges Pompidou was in all likelihood no more anti-Semitic than his mentor de Gaulle. Before entering politics, he had been a director of the Banque Rothschild. Early in his presidency, and most controversially, he pardoned Paul Touvier, in prison for murdering Jews in the war, and who would almost certainly have been executed if Catholic priests had not hidden him and so enabled him to escape justice for several decades. He is on record telling the journalist Philippe de Saint-Robert (admittedly a latter-day Drumont) that the then-Israeli ambassador to Paris, Asher Ben-Natan, was "the perfect prototype of a Nazi officer." (Asked to comment after his tour of duty on Franco-Israeli relations, Ben-Natan answered, "They cannot get any worse. France has pushed the help it gives to the Palestinians to the very limit.") The Israelis, Pompidou further elaborated to Saint-Robert, were "mad. They don't see the world as it is, not even the Arab world. Or else they don't want peace."

Pompidou, it is true, was humiliated in a most public way by one of Israel's memorably spectacular coups. Israel had paid for twelve fast patrol boats armed with missiles and taken delivery of seven, but five had been caught by the embargo. At the very end of 1969, Israeli sailors infiltrated Cherbourg harbor, slipped on board the boats, and headed at full speed for Israel. Arafat complained that he could not understand why the French navy and air force had taken no action to recover the boats. Only weeks later, Pompidou paid a state visit to the United States. In a speech he said that Israel must cease being "a racial and religious state" in order to assimilate with the rest of the Middle East. In Chicago he further demanded that Israel refrain from appealing for support from Jews in other countries. A crowd of infuriated Jews mobbed Pompidou and his wife at the Palmer House Hotel, shouting "Shame on you, Pompidou." President Nixon duly flew in to soothe the rattled Pompidous. Golda Meir, the Israeli prime minister, however, commented that the French president had shown Israel how to commit suicide.

Diplomacy, Pompidou's successor Valéry Giscard d'Estaing asserted, is "a matter of intuition," and "the art of the moment." Probably he too had nothing personal either against Israel or Jews, yet his presidency from

1974 to 1981 intensified the harm done to them, and, correspondingly, the favoring of Arabs. At the outset of his term in office, he said to a senior official of the Quai d'Orsay, "I am the real minister of foreign affairs." At that same time, the Quai d'Orsay put out a statement in the idiom of the PLO, to the effect that a just and lasting peace in the Middle East had to satisfy the legitimate aspirations of the Palestinian people. In a move amounting to official recognition, Giscard sent his foreign minister Jean Sauvagnargues to Lebanon for a meeting with Arafat in the former palace of the High Commissioner, now the French embassy. Sauvagnargues addressed Arafat as "Mr. President" and in a press conference called him a "moderate" with "the stature of a statesman."

The Abu Daoud incident reveals that for the sake of PLO good will France was ready to dispense with the law as well as its obligations to another European country, never mind Israel. Abu Daoud was a terrorist at the head of Black September, the group responsible for the murder of Israeli Olympic athletes in 1972. The French embassy in Beirut gave him a visa, and he arrived in Paris in the first days of 1977. On January 7, accompanied by the PLO representative, he visited the Quai d'Orsay, where Pierre Serles, head of the North Africa and Middle East department, received him. Some hours later, he was arrested through Interpol. The German government wanted him to be extradited and tried for his role in the Munich atrocity. In their account of this affair, the Arab historians Samir Kassir and Farouk Mardam-Bey state that the Quai d'Orsay informed Arab ambassadors that it was in the dark about everything. Mysteriously, Abu Daoud was freed by a judge four days later, and instantly released to Algeria. The Quai d'Orsay then apologized to the PLO representative for the arrest in the first place. Amid recrimination all round, Israel accused the government of cowardice and recalled its ambassador, Mordecai Gazit. On January 17, Giscard thought to rebut all criticism by saying, "France and its people have no lessons to learn from anyone."

The 1973 war had deepened fault-lines already apparent among the Cold War allies against the Soviet Union. Giscard played the countries of the EU off against the United States and Israel. Shortly before Sadat's historic visit to Jerusalem, France pushed the other Europeans to declare that a *patrie* was among the legitimate rights of the Palestinians—the first time that word, freighted with French history, had appeared in a European Community document. The aim was clearly to align Europe with Arab countries fiercely rejecting Sadat's initiative. In spoiler's language once again identical to the PLO's, Giscard criticized the peace between Egypt and Israel sealed at Camp David in 1978. Besides repudiating pressure to abstain from finalizing the contracts for the Iraqi nuclear plant, Giscard sought to replace the weakening Soviet Union as a supplier of conventional arms to the Arabs. At the time, the French historian Pierre Nora observed that French Jews were coming to support Israel more and more unconditionally and criticizing their own government more and more systematically. In a study of the role of Jews in French politics, Maurice

Szafran speaks of "open war" between the Jews and Giscard.

Foreign ministers from Couve de Murville, Michel Jobert, Louis de Guiringaud, and Jean François-Poncet to Sauvagnargues, uniformly supported appeasement of Arab states as a central plank of French policy. Of them all, the most single-minded was Jobert. Born in Morocco, he spoke fluent Arabic and once wrote a novel in the Paul Morand style, with disobliging Jewish characters, set in his home-town of Meknès. He was Pompidou's director general at the Elysée before taking over the Quai d'Orsay in 1973. French foreign policy, as Jobert sought to explain and justify, was not pro-Arab but simply "active, a just reflection of the interests of France" in the Arab part of the world. The Near East, he also wrote, had traditionally "turned towards Anglo-Saxon culture and commerce," and "our industrialists, our businessmen, our professors" should now supplant them.

When Egypt and Syria sprang their surprise attack on Israel that October, Jobert commented, "Is it unexpected aggression to try and set foot in your own house?"— though quite how Israel belonged to the house of Egypt or Syria he did not explain. Illustrating Jobert's emotional stance against Israel, the journalist Jean-Louis Remilleux in his book *Ni Dieu ni diable* quotes him saying flatly, "I will not go to Jerusalem." So blatant was his bias that one cartoonist drew him wearing Arab slippers and trampling on the Israeli flag, while Raymond Aron described him as a dwarf "perched on the scaffolding of his set-backs." In *Les Illusions immobiles,* a collection of self-justificatory journalism published in 1999, Jobert expressed the French view now entrenched in Brussels, that Europe has a "vocation" to oppose "the double aberration of Israel and the United States" which can only lead to "oriental upheavals prejudicial to it."

A Thirties fascist and then a Vichy official, a Gaullist supporter and finally a socialist, François Mitterrand was politically, morally, and personally corrupt. The fourteen years of his presidency from 1981 to 1995 carried the stamp of his opportunistic personality and his cynical intelligence. As *Le Monde* was to put it, he quickly demonstrated "his talents for trickery [*la ruse*]." Earlier in his life, in 1949, he had visited the Jerusalem holy sites then in Jordanian hands, and he now let it be known that he intended to restore good relations with Israel. He covered himself, however, as his secretary Jacques Attali records in his diary *Verbatim*, by ordering his foreign policy aides, Hubert Védrine (a future foreign minister and himself the son of a high-ranking Vichy official) and Claude de Kémoularia, to do the rounds of Arab embassies in Paris and proffer them the sophistry that "Good contact between France and Israel will be in your interest." Mitterrand's double-faced approach was exemplified in his condemnation of the destruction by Israel of the Iraqi Osirak nuclear plant in 1981 and his flattering address to the Knesset some months later; his airy proposal of a federation of Jordan, Israel, and Palestine, and his incompatible role in preserving Arafat from the consequences of his campaigns of violence from the Beirut debacle in 1982 and for the rest of the decade.

With characteristic equivocation, Mitterrand maintained the Quai d'Orsay as Europe's foremost official pro-Arab and anti-Israel lobby, packing it with cronies. Kémoularia, entrusted with confidential matters, had close connections to Saudi Arabia. For the first three years of Mitterrand's term, the foreign minister was Claude Cheysson, and the pair of them tugged in different directions. France's foreign policy, Cheysson explained to an interviewer soon after he had taken office, was in the hands of the President, the Prime Minister, and the principal Quai d'Orsay ministers: "What anyone else says has no significance." His hostility to Israel stemmed in part from his experience as a United Nations observer in the 1948 fighting, and in part from his friendship with PLO representatives such as Naim Khadir in Brussels. While he was at the Quai d'Orsay, Arafat's colleagues danced a "tireless" ("*inlassable*") ballet in his office, in the image of one historian. The murder of Egyptian President Anwar Sadat in 1981 was positive, in an opinon the Cheysson was alone to hold among Western foreign ministers, because it would "unblock the situation," as though peace with Israel would block it. "My condemnation of Zionism is absolute," he was to tell the Franco-Palestinian Medical Association once he was no longer minister. "The state of Israel created itself against the will of the rest of the world."

Roland Dumas, a lawyer by training, followed Cheysson in 1984. Opposed to the 1956 Suez campaign, and a prominent defender in the courts of FLN members fighting for independence, he was well known as a particular friend of Algerians and Palestinians. Within three months of taking office, he visited Arafat in Tunis, where the latter had taken refuge after the forced evacuation from Beirut. A lawyer, Dumas had advised the defense in the case of Monsignor Hilarion Capucci, a Greek Orthodox priest caught gun-running for the PLO, and he played the leading role in ensuring that the terrorist Abu Daoud was hurried out of the country. "Air piracy," he was to tell a newspaper in December 1984, "was the only way for Palestinian resistance to smash international indifference." At the time of the first Gulf War, Agence France Presse reported that he had expressed "the sympathy of France" to the appropriate Saudi prince for the dozen Scud missiles that Saddam Hussein had fired on Riyadh and Dhahran but had nothing to say about the many more Scuds fired at Israel. (Years later, he and his mistress Christine Deviers-Joncour were to be central figures in the scandal involving misappropriation of funds from Elf-Aquitaine, the national oil company.)

Under Cheysson, the Quai d'Orsay's director general was Francis Gutmann, an unusual appointment because he was parachuted into the ministry from his previous job with the Red Cross. A colleague of Jobert's, he had impeccable Arabist credentials, however. It fell to him to manage the salvaging of Arafat and the PLO once the Israelis had cornered them in Beirut in 1982. Bertrand Dufourcq, another influential Arabist, had been in the cabinets of Couve de Murville, Cheysson, and Dumas before he too became director general of the Quai d'Orsay. When the Israelis captured P L O documents in Beirut in 1982, they found evidence that French diplomats or their informers in Tel Aviv and Damascus had been leaking information about the operation to the P L O. In 1987, it emerged that the Quai d'Orsay was subsidizing an Arab lobby, the Cercle France–Pays Arabes. In his diaries *Mission piégée*, the then Israeli ambassador Ovadia Soffer sums up the attitude of the Quai d'Orsay: "The coldness was glacial."

THIRTEEN

Interests and Hearts

THE POLICY OUTLINE of France towards the Middle East since 1967, then, has been imperialism in modern guise. The modern age, however, cultivates a doctrine of abhorring imperialism and anything that smacks of it. Those who have determined French policy have therefore unanimously pretended to the lofty aim of facilitating peace between Arabs and Israelis while taking decisions that hinder the realization of such peace, but more meaningfully serve to gain power and influence and money for themselves.

The first Arab one-man ruler to attract avid attention in post-de Gaulle Paris was Mu'ammer Gaddhafi who had seized power in a coup in Libya in 1969. He was an unknown quantity, and his country's oil wealth was tantalizing. France immediately sold him a hundred and ten Mirage aircraft destined for Israel but blocked by the embargo. Hervé Alphand, secretary general of the Quai d'Orsay at the time, noted in his diary that the resale of these aircraft, for which Israel had already paid, was upsetting public opinion at home and abroad, but he himself pushed for it as "it is nonetheless in the normal line of our Arab and Mediterranean policy."

A more amenable Arab leader than the erratic Gaddhafi was Yasser Arafat. The wars of 1967 and 1973 had left no scope for military victory to resolve the Israeli-Arab confrontation on the absolute terms for which the Arabs had fought. In the eyes of the Arab leaders any negotiation with Israel was tantamount to accepting defeat, and they rejected any such approach. Here was an opening for the Palestinians to take matters into their own hands and Arafat was quick to exploit it. Small and chubby, boosting his unmilitary image by wearing an Arab headdress and failing to shave, his wits were his chief asset. A notable self-publicist, he was skilled in telling interlocutors what they wanted to hear. Promising to be helpful to Soviet interests and harmful to the United States, he succeeded in persuading Leonid Brezhnev and the Politburo to arm and sponsor the Palestine Liberation Organization. At the same time, and on much the same anti-American grounds, he persuaded the French to become his principal civilian sponsors in the international arena. Arafat and the PLO thus formed an unusual Franco-Soviet compound that enlarged what had been in its origins a regional border dispute into one of the most intractable issues of the age, with international ramifications. Escalating from guerrilla tactics to general terrorism, Arafat made it unmistakably clear that the long-term goal was to uproot and scatter the Jews of Israel. From bases first in Jordan and then in Lebanon, he instead provoked civil wars that left thousands of fellow Arabs dead, further tyrannizing an already tyrannized Middle East.

France, in the perception of its policy-makers, was to be the mediator for a dispute that the parties in the region could never resolve for themselves. So they shaped a policy designed to prove that they were right. Morality, justice, fact—they were no obstacle. In the United Nations, France inverted reality to argue that the Palestinians were not the cause of war in the Middle East but the key to peace. In 1972, inspired by France, the UN passed a vote accusing Israel of violating the Geneva Convention and committing war crimes in the occupied territories. In October 1974, France scored another diplomatic success by steering through a vote that the PLO should have representation in the UN Assembly. Soon afterwards, amid standing applause and wearing the khaki battle-dress that he affected complete with holster and revolver, Arafat addressed the UN, and delegates from countries that in living memory had murdered Jews next passed the resolution that Zionism was racism. Here was "a confusion of terms," in the oddly cerebral phrase of Louis de Guiringaud, French representative at the General Assembly.

France then refused to support President Anwar Sadat in the historic break-through that led to peace between Egypt and Israel. Opposition to the Camp David agreement that finalized this peace was grounded in the sole reason that France was evidently no sort of mediator but had been entirely excluded from the whole process. Worse still, parties in the region were evidently able to come to a peace agreement by themselves.

France was able to exert further but different pressure in Brussels, the capital of the countries in the process of amalgamating the continent into the empire of the European Union. In November 1973, France persuaded the other members to pass a declaration calling for Israeli withdrawal from all the occupied territories, thus removing the ambiguity carefully crafted in UN Resolution 242 which referred to "territories" without the definite article. Two years later, French policy specified that the Palestinians had the right to a *patrie*, or homeland, in this instance a term symmetrical to the original Balfour Declaration on behalf of a Jewish homeland. Homeland soon developed into "self-determination."

In 1979 the European Community (as it still was) adopted the French view and decided to sponsor the PLO henceforth, ever since remaining its most faithful supporter and provider of financial aid no matter what acts of terror the PLO committed. The following year, France masterminded the so-called Venice Declaration of the countries in the European Community, whereby the PLO was to be the instrument of this self-determination. Reality as usual caught up with illusion, when Israel entered Lebanon in strength in 1982, in order to close down the terrorism organized and launched there by the PLO. France sent ships to Beirut to evacuate thousands of

PLO gunmen to Tunis, and Paul-Marc Henry, the French ambassador to Lebanon, placed Arafat under the cover of his own diplomatic immunity.

One of de Gaulle's last acts had been to consent to the presence in Paris of Fatah, Arafat's terrorist arm. The director general of the Quai d'Orsay, Geoffroy de Courcel, then arranged with Khalid al-Hassan, a confidential advisor of Arafat's, to enlarge this into an office for the PLO, the overall political arm of the cause. This immediately reproduced on French streets the brutal politics of the Middle East. Mahmud Hamshari, the PLO representative, was gunned down in December 1972, and died soon afterwards. His office turned out to be a weapons depot and a communication center. His successor, Mahmud Saleh, was also assassinated. In October 1980, PLO terrorists killed four Jews and wounded thirty more in the Rue Copernic; again, in August 1982 in the Rue des Rosiers, they killed six Jews and injured twenty-two. (On the former occasion, Raymond Barre, then prime minister, said that "two innocent French people were killed" as well, which put the dead Jews well and truly in their place, as far as he was concerned). Not so far in the future, Paris was to suffer terror attacks from Algerian Islamists, and to frustrate others from al-Qaeda or similar groups. The protracted series of outrages includes the explosion of a booby-trapped car outside the premises of a pro-Iraqi paper (for which Syria was almost certainly responsible), and the murders performed or attempted by Ilich Ramirez Sanchez, otherwise the Jackal (for which ultimate responsibility is hard to pin down among his various Arab sponsors). In the summer of 1975, Sanchez shot dead two detectives who were arresting him in Paris, whereupon he escaped to Beirut. Almost twenty years later, however, he was handed over by the Sudanese authorities, tried in France, and sentenced to life imprisonment. At the end of June 1976, an Air France Airbus was hijacked to Entebbe in Uganda, and its passengers held hostage until Israeli commandos rescued them with spectacular daring. Such major outrages, as well as the regular bombings of French embassies and offices in Arab countries, have made a dead letter of the "gentleman's agreement" Pompidou thought he had negotiated with the PLO, indeed of all similar attempts to curry favor with one or another Arab or Muslim one-man ruler.

A subsequent PLO representative in Paris, Ibrahim Souss, was Arafat's brother-in-law; they had both married daughters of Raimonda Tawil, a society lady in Nablus. *Paris, Capitale Arabe*, by Nicolas Beau, describes how Souss, allegedly a good pianist, was "appreciated in fashionable drawing rooms, where this French-speaking intellectual enjoyed formidable popularity." According to this source, Souss influenced Hubert Védrine, general secretary at the Elysée and later Foreign Minister. The then-foreign minister, Jean-Bernard Raimond, invited Souss at meetings with Arab ambassadors, thus seeming to rank him with representatives of states. Lionel Jospin, the Socialist Prime Minister, further invited him to Socialist Party congresses. In the gathering atmosphere of mutual embrace—with undertones of blackmail on the part of the Arabs—the Pompidou government was eventually able to negotiate a "gentleman's agreement" specifying that the PLO would neither attack Israeli interests in France nor hijack Air France planes.

President Giscard d'Estaing invited Arafat on a first official visit to Paris. In November 1979, a grand reception was held for him in the Elysée. The Israeli ambassador, Meir Rosenne, asked, "Would France invite Hitler?" (Hitler after all had needed no inviting to enter France with armed forces.) Sion de Leusse, director general of the Quai d'Orsay, accused Rosenne of having "outraged" France, after which the ambassador remained, as the historian Howard Sachar dryly puts it, "virtually a non-person in French official circles." Another official visit of Arafat to the Elysée followed in May 1989, during the course of which he pronounced that the clauses of the PLO Charter calling for the destruction of Israel were "*caduc*"—a legalism meaning "fallen by the way." At the time the expression was presented as a breakthrough, but events were to prove that this unexpected mastery of the French language masked deception. The peace process that had dragged out exhaustively from the Oslo Accords to the second Camp David meeting under the auspices of President Clinton led only to the sustained and deliberate violence of another intifada.

Consolidating a privileged position in Saudi Arabia since the end of the Second World War, the United States had shut France out of participating in Aramco, with its oil monopoly in the country. Iraq possessed reserves of oil second only to Saudi Arabia. The country had once been in the British sphere, but after the revolution of 1958 became dangerously unstable as contenders for power veered between Arab nationalism and subjection to the Soviet Communist bloc. Playing up its well-established support of Arab nationalism, France stood to gain economically. Politically, France hoped that a French-dominated Iraq would come to rival the American-dominated Saudi Arabia.

Jacques Chirac will be remembered as the politician who more than anyone else committed France to aid and abet Iraq, regardless of the murderous harm done in the process over many years to Iraqis themselves and to their neighbors, aggravated by the promotion of instability in the world at large. His career began in the governments of de Gaulle and Pompidou, and he became prime minister under Giscard as well as Mitterrand. Elected President in 1995, he seemed to express the need for grandeur and prestige characteristic of the French elite of which he was such a prime and enduring representative. In the arenas of the United Nations and the European Union, he deployed the full range of his skills and his experience to arm and strengthen this most brutal dictatorship, committing France to defend publicly what was always indefensible, in flagrant opposition to the humane values for which the country has credited itself since 1789.

The Baath Party seized power in Baghdad in a coup in 1968, and immediately murdered as many Communists as possible. From the outset, Saddam Hussein, the strongman of the Baath, made it plain that he would stop at nothing in pursuit of absolute power; only a few short years were to pass before he eliminated other contenders to become president and one-man ruler. The weakening of the Soviet hold offered the French the prospect of interposing themselves and acquiring a client state with a need to sell its oil and to purchase weaponry. Pierre Serles, at that time the ambassador in Baghdad, helped to lay the foundations of friendship with Iraq. Saddam rarely traveled abroad, but paid an official visit to Paris in June 1972. In *Le Livre noir de Saddam Hussein,* Chris Kutschera relates how Saddam lured Jacques Chaban-Delmas, the French prime minister, saying, "We open the door to France with the invitation to profit from the opportunity we are offering. It will be as much in your interest as ours."

Bernard Kouchner, founder of the organization Doctors without Borders, went to the aid of the Kurds as they were being forced by Saddam to flee from their homes in November 1974, and found himself under attack from helicopters and missiles manufactured in his native France, prompting him to reflect, also in *Le Livre noir*, that his country was selling Saddam the means of death (*"Notre pays lui vendait de la mort"*).

In the course of a preliminary meeting in Baghdad, Jacques Chirac, successor of Chaban-Delmas as prime minister, lost no time forming a mutual admiration society with Saddam Hussein. In every sense, whether political or intellectual or human, the conjuncture was unnatural. Chirac had served as a junior officer in Algeria in the 1950s and was in no sense an admirer of Arab nationalism. (Completing a volte-face, in March 2003 he was to lay a wreath at the monument in Algiers to "martyrs" who had fought the French.) Although nominally a right-wing Gaullist, he could declaim to his new friend, "National-ism in the best sense of the word, and socialism as the means of mobilizing energies and organizing tomorrow's society, are sentiments very close to French hearts." In 1975 Saddam returned to France on two occasions, in March and in September, when Chirac gushed, "I wel-come you as my personal friend. I assure you of my esteem, my consideration, and my affection," explaining that "impulses of the heart" dictated policy as much as national interest did. They finalized the purchase of air-craft, and Chirac then accompanied his guest on a tour of a nuclear research center in Provence, offering to sell Saddam a nuclear reactor similar to the one sold to Israel some eighteen years previously. French technicians would supervise this Osirak project, and the French gov-ernment agreed without demur to the Iraqi condition that none of them would be "persons of the Jewish race or the Mosaic religion." Apparently nobody paused to query the morality of supplying atomic weapons to par-ties who might annihilate one another with them. Non-proliferation treaties were evidently also of no account. An anxious Washington asked President Giscard to re-consider, only to receive this brush-off: "We cannot let our American and European allies continue their offen-sive against our nuclear industry."

Within a year, Chirac and Raymond Barre, then Prime Minister, called on Saddam in Baghdad. Contracts were signed for more weaponry, an airport, desalination

plants, cars, all worth billions of dollars, with oil concessions thrown in as sweeteners. Israel did what it could
to impede the finalization of the nuclear reactor, but by
1981 the plant was about to become active, whereupon
an attack on it had to be excluded in consideration of the
dire human consequences. That June, in a sortie com-
bining technical excellence and daring, eight Israeli aircraft reduced the reactor to a burnt-out wreck. The sole
human casualty was one of the French technicians, by
the name of Damien Chassepied, who unknown to the
French or the Iraqis had been secretly helping the Israeli
squadron to navigate to the target, lingered a little too
long on the site, and so lost his life in a feat for which at
least some of the credit was his. Though this could not be
appreciated at the time, the raid put paid to Saddam's
ambitions to be some sort of Arab Bismarck. Armed with
the nuclear weapon, he might well have been able to
subject his neighbors to his absolute rule.

Some months after the Israeli strike, Foreign Minister
Claude Cheysson appears to have told Tariq Aziz, Saddam's titular Foreign Minister, that France would replace
the destroyed reactor. In Baghdad in 1982, Cheysson
finalized an arms deal incorporating Exocet missiles
worth fifteen billion francs. Contracts were under discus-
sion for even more staggering sums. At a critical moment
in the Iraq-Iran war, France furnished Saddam with five
Super-Etendards belonging to its own standing forces.
On December 1, 1989, General Jacques Mitterrand of
the French Corps of Military Engineers went to Baghdad

with a personal message from his brother, President François Mitterrand, promising "political support." Jacques Mitterrand and Jean-Pierre Chevènement, Minister of Defense and an avowed admirer of Saddam, were to co-ordinate the details of Franco-Iraqi military co-operation.

Saddam's invasion of Kuwait in August 1990 embarrassingly interrupted this cosiness. As the well-known commentator Dominique Moisi put it, the President is the true interpreter of foreign policy, inevitably personalizing it and so reinforcing in this crisis a sense of marginalization in the Quai d'Orsay. In a speech to the UN General Assembly, President Mitterrand pretended that some of Saddam's claims on Kuwait were legitimate. In recompense, Saddam released the 327 French people that among those of many other nationalities he had been holding hostage. Evidently he expected France somehow to rescue him from the war that loomed. Chevènement held that the Allied coalition was waging "a colonial war." Balking finally, France instead joined the Allied coalition, even sending an aircraft carrier to the Gulf, though without the Super-Etendard attack aircraft it normally carried. Jean-François Revel, one of France's most trenchant writers, was prompted to make the wise-crack that the national contribution should have been to send the famous Bluebell girls to dance on the empty flight deck. The national see-sawing between a sense of superiority and a sense of inferiority towards the United States was memorably captured when at that moment of crisis Mitterrand said that nobody dictated to France, continuing, "I respect Mr. Bush but I do not feel myself to be in the position of a second-class private obliged to obey his commander-in-chief."

FOURTEEN

The Pursuit of the Ayatollah

Ayatollah Ruhollah Khomeini flew into Paris on 6 October 1977, accompanied by his wife and faithful collaborators. Iranian critics of their Shah, some of them religious and others secular intellectuals completely at ease in French left-wing circles, met him, and eventually found him quarters at Neauphle-le-Château, a *banlieue* with easy access to Paris. The Ayatollah had two somewhat nondescript houses at his disposal, and in the garden a blue and white tent was rigged up where he could lead prayers.

In exile from Iran since 1963, he had been first in Turkey and then in Iraq, at Najaf, one of the great centers of Shia devotion. There he had made a reputation for himself as a Shia traditionalist, but he had also declared uncompromising opposition to Mohammad Reza Pahlavi, the Shah, unleashing the vitriolic anger and scorn of which he was a master. Regular demonstrations with occasional loss of life duly swelled towards a crescendo of revolution, and so the Shah requested Saddam Hussein to expel the Ayatollah. Syria and Kuwait then refused to accept him. Khomeini had never lived outside a Muslim country, and sought refuge in France because there seemed nowhere else to go. A visa was a formality. In Khomeini's own words, "To begin with, the French government was a bit cautious. But then they were kind to us and we could publicize our views extensively, much more so than we expected." In return, he was utterly indifferent to France and its culture, never once visiting the sights of Paris. To him, the city was "the capital of the Franks."

In his memoirs, *Answer to History*, the Shah has described how President Giscard sent a personal envoy to Tehran to advocate a "political solution to the crisis," which he rightly considered a euphemism for rejection of the use of force against the gathering Shia militancy. This envoy seems to have been the head of French intelligence, Comte Alexandre de Marenches. Christian Delannoy and Jean-Pierre Pichard in their book *Khomeini: La Révolution trahie* at any rate quote the Shah deluding himself in conversation with the visiting Marenches, "If you don't keep Khomeini in France, he will go to Damascus." Here, then, was an open invitation to the French to make of Khomeini what they would. Mir Ali Asghar Montazem, an Iranian critical of both Khomeini and the French, puts it more forcefully in his book *The Life and Times of Ayatollah Khomeini*: "Some sources claim that French intelligence wanted Khomeini admitted to the country because he was seen as Iran's future leader, others credit the French Foreign Ministry with this foresight." The eminent and authoritative Iranian journalist Amir Taheri, soon to be an exile himself, is explicit in his book *The Spirit of Allah*, writing that the French were the first to be persuaded that a government under Khomeini would offer them "a golden opportunity in Iran."

Tall and gaunt, his ascetic appearance enhanced by black robes and a heavy turban, Khomeini at once attracted the world's attention as he vituperated daily against the Shah and the infidel United States that would have to pay dearly for supporting the royal oppressor of his people. In contrast, he gave assurances that under him Iran would be a free society, and he hinted at democracy, equality and rights, even for women, though naturally qualified in accordance with Islam. Neauphle-le-Château became at the same time a media extravaganza and a center of subversion, the one aspect feeding the other. Always with his eye on the main chance, President Mitterrand proposed to call on the Ayatollah, but then did not do so. Amir Taheri calculates that in the four months of his stay the Ayatollah gave 132 radio, television, and press interviews, and published fifty declarations—some French sources give much higher figures. He also received almost one hundred thousand Iranians, who between them contributed donations of more than £20 million, much of it in cash. Muhammad Hassanein Heikal, the Egyptian journalist and once Nasser's confidant, was one of those granted an interview, and he has recorded how the local gendarmes had handed the Ayatollah's body-guards permits for a limited number of weapons, including two machine-guns. The Palestinians, he adds without commenting on the legality of it, provided yet more arms.

The use of French communications more than anything else consummated the downfall of the Shah's regime. The local post office put at Khomeini's disposal two telexes and six telephone lines, enabling him to issue instructions and manipulate violence while himself remaining safely beyond the Shah's reach. Fereydoun Hoveyda, brother of the Shah's luckless Prime Minister Amir Abbas Hoveyda (first sacrificed by the Shah and then judicially murdered by the Ayatollah), has noted how in palace circles there was astonishment at the attitude of the French government, "which was allowing the exiled cleric to incite a rebellion, contrary to the international rules governing political refugees."

Charles Chayet of the Quai d'Orsay was the official liaising with Neauphle-le-Château. He seems to have been in two minds. At the very beginning of January 1979, he informed Khomeini that he was about to overstay the three months allowed to a tourist, and would have to apply for a resident's permit, otherwise he would be obliged to leave the country. Chayet presented a memorandum on this matter to President Giscard, and he in turn handed it to President Carter at a summit meeting previously arranged on the French West Indian island of Guadeloupe. Hardly more than a year earlier, Carter had publicly celebrated the Shah's reign, received him on a state visit to Washington, and fulsomely praised him as enjoying "his people's total confidence." That

December, a bare month before the Guadeloupe meeting, Carter had complained to Giscard about the destabilizing presence of Khomeini in Neauphle-le-Château. Reversing himself abruptly at Guadeloupe, he said that the United States would now not oppose any new government in Iran as long as representative elections were held. Chayet duly relayed to Khomeini the news that the United States and France were prepared to accept him in place of the Shah. Yet in his autobiography *Keeping Faith*, Carter describes one more twist of uncertainty, claiming that he called Giscard on January 14, 1979, to ask him to do everything to delay the Ayatollah's imminent departure to take power in Iran.

Too late. By that date, the Ayatollah had unconditional victory in his grasp. The Shah fled. On February 1, Khomeini himself was flying from Paris to Tehran on an Air France charter plane, on arrival descending the steps from the aircraft with an Air France pilot supporting him. Carter's equivocating and inept zigzag of policy towards Iran had set the seal on a revolution with repercussions for the world as perilous as any of the great revolutions of history. Installed with absolute authority over every aspect of the state, the Ayatollah repudiated the freedoms he had so often promised in interviews and broadcasts at Neauphle-le-Château. One of his disciples there, one in fact described as his "spiritual son," had been Abol Hasan Bani Sadr, at first appointed president but soon forced to flee back to Paris in fear of his life. He quotes Khomeini as saying, "In Paris, I found it opportune to say what I said. In Iran, I find it opportune to deny it, and I deny it

quite frankly." During the war with Iraq, this grim auto-
crat imported half a million small plastic keys from Tai-
wan and issued them to schoolchildren supposedly to
open the gates of paradise as they blew themselves up,
ordered to walk unarmed over Iraqi minefields. In a span
of rule more cruel and absolute than the Shah's, the Ayatollah transformed Iran into a country with a mission in
the name of Islam to challenge unbelievers everywhere,
galvanizing Iranians and Muslims in other countries to
confront and subdue the United States and the West,
whose peoples are to be perceived primarily as Christians and Jews. A clash of civilizations has become a real
prospect, and, should it prove a reality, the France of
Mitterrand and Giscard will have done much to bring it
about.

Since the days of Napoleon Bonaparte, France has
resented the influence of the British and the Russians in
Persia (as it then was), and sent military and cultural
missions in the attempt to alter the balance of power in
its favor. Sweeping Iran after Khomeini's return, rabid
and official anti-Americanism appeared to offer renewed
prospects to the French, on the grounds that one's
enemy's enemy is one's friend. This proved yet another
self-deception within months. In September 1980, Saddam Hussein launched a war with Iran that was to last
eight years at great cost to both countries. A principal
supplier of arms to Iraq, France nevertheless engaged in
surreptitious sales of arms to Iran.

Out to establish that France could not have things
both ways, the Iranians and their agents undertook a

campaign of terror lasting through the 1980s, abetted by the PLO that was oblivious to any putative "gentleman's agreement" about renouncing violence against France. Introducing the terrorist organization Hizbollah into Lebanon and Syria, Iran was able to extend its reach into the Arab world while disclaiming that it was doing so. Among the numerous Iranians escaping to Paris from the Khomeini regime was Shapour Bakhtiar, a former Prime Minister. In a botched attempt to murder him in July 1980 in his house in Neuilly, the killers shot a policeman and a passing woman. (Bakhtiar was in fact murdered some years later, and Mitterrand was to surrender to Iranian demands and pardon the four men convicted of the earlier attempt at assassination.)

In retaliation, or perhaps to demonstrate their power, on September 4, 1981 gun-men, either hired Syrians or from Hizbollah, shot dead Louis Delamarre, French ambassador in Beirut. Two years later, Hizbollah suicide bombers drove into the compound where French peace-keeping troops were quartered, killing fifty-eight. That year, too, the French embassy in Kuwait was bombed, and in 1984 Guy Georgy, the ambassador in Tehran, was taken hostage (much as American diplomats had been held hostage in response to Carter's overtures) and released only in exchange for an Iranian master-terrorist due to be tried in Paris. Six French citizens, two of them from the embassy, were kidnapped in Beirut in 1985 and held for two years. One of them, Michel Seurat, was murdered, and his remains returned to his widow only in 2006. In assorted bombings in Paris, including on the

Champs Elysées and the Boulevard Saint-Michel, as well as in the rue de Rennes, at least eleven people were killed and 163 wounded. In addition, Iranian agents killed seventeen Iranian exiles or dissidents in France, according to Amir Taheri's compilation. When judges in 1987 sought to interrogate one Wahid Gordji of the Iranian embassy, Iran broke off diplomatic relations, a move in stark contrast to the supine acceptance by the French of the physical violence done to Guy Georgy in Tehran. After back-channel negotiations and humiliating concessions on the part of the French, relations were restored a year later.

President Mitterrand lamented, "We are not the enemies of Iran.... Iraq is a friendly country. But I cannot accept that our arms sales can be considered an act of aggression.... France has not chosen its camp; it happens to have a friendship, and does not wish to have an enemy." This impasse, these contradictions, were the outcome of a chain of officially inspired events summarized by the journalist Pierre Péan as mixing in variable doses "cowardice, contempt, incompetence, frivolity and *raison d'état.*" This handling of Khomeini was a repeat of the handling more than thirty years earlier of Haj Amin, the Mufti of Jerusalem, equally futile in the search for aggrandizement and equally threatening to stability in the Middle East, Europe, and beyond.

FIFTEEN

Ins and Some Outs

THE QUAI D'ORSAY today is responsible for 252 embassies and consulates, according to official figures, a total just eight fewer than the United States, whose population is many times larger and whose interests are far wider and more international. Representation on this scale is intended to amass influence and prestige, in the Middle East above all.

To expound its Muslim and Arab policy, the Quai d'Orsay has always treated *Le Monde*, a newspaper of prestige, as its semi-official channel. A yet more powerful outlet is Agence France Presse, one of the world's handful of leading press agencies, with offices in some 150 countries and over 10,000 media outlets. In theory AFP is independent but in practice the government controls a large shareholding in it. The Prime Minister, the Foreign Minister, and the Finance Minister each have the right to appoint a member of the board of eight, while two of the other five in a vague definition have to be men "who have represented France abroad." The Quai d'Orsay is thus well placed to treat AFP as what one critic has called "a strategic instrument," supervizing and guiding the flow of information.

Further protecting its hold on informed opinion, the state pays half the budget of the French Institute for International Relations, known by its acronym as IFR, and perhaps the most prominent think-tank for foreign affairs. On its board are two former foreign ministers, Hubert Védrine and Michel Barnier, and also Luc Debieuvre (formerly director of an Arab bank in Paris) who is on record saying that "the Middle East policy of the U.S. is made in Israel and not in Washington." Pascal Boniface, the director of the Institute of International and Strategic Relations (its acronym is IRIS), a think-tank sponsored by the Ministry for European Affairs, caused a scandal in 2000 when he warned that "the Arab-Muslim community" would resent an even-handed policy in the Middle East as an injustice. By supporting Israel, he added with more than an edge of menace, Jews were too greatly isolating themselves. In self-defense, he claimed to be expressing official policy. The Quai d'Orsay and the Ministry of Culture subsidized the Franco-Egyptian production of the film *La Porte du soleil* for Arte, the public service television channel. The film presents the 1948 war as nothing but a series of massacres of Arab civilians committed by the Jews. The Quai d'Orsay further promoted this fictionalization of history on its web-site.

In contrast to the foreign policy establishment and its

determination to act and speak as though the national interest demanded siding with the Muslim Middle East in all its issues and prejudices, public opinion in France has been in the main supportive of Israel and Jews generally, while wary of a *"France musulmane."* Even within the establishment, a few rare spirits manage to break the conceptual fetters binding their colleagues. As ambassador in Israel for much of the 1950s, Pierre Gilbert—as we have seen—played an important part in ensuring the provision of French armaments to Israel. It was much noted at the time that in a gesture of solidarity he accompanied Ben-Gurion to the airfield where new Mystères were being delivered from France. Openly and exceptionally pro-Zionist, he had the courage to stand up to de Gaulle. One of Couve de Murville's first acts as Foreign Minister was to sack him.

Replacing Gilbert, Jean Bourdeillette was ambassador from 1959 to 1965, and no less exceptionally pro-Zionist. At a meeting with de Gaulle a few days before taking up his post, he insisted on the implementation of a Franco-Israeli cultural agreement that had been signed but remained a dead letter. De Gaulle gave the order to proceed. Bourdeillette's memoirs, *Pour Israël*, are a tribute to the independence of his mind, even containing a chapter in praise of the Israeli army, singling out "the determination, the calm courage, the stoical resignation" of the soldiers, and the modesty and lack of militarism in the generals. Christianity, he observes, had deformed the Jewish people, and now in Paris, "Israel was sacrificed to the linked exigencies of two policies, the one anti-

American and the other pro-Arab." To him, the hostile attitude adopted by the elite towards Israel was nothing less than "our Dreyfus affair."

Henri Froment-Meurice describes with pride in his autobiography, *Vu du Quai*, how he was promoted to the fourth floor of the ministry, from where the view over the sights of Paris was "sublime." His grandmother and her sister, née Ullmann from Frankfort, were saved from the Germans during the war, he writes, because they had a certificate showing that their father had been baptized a Catholic. He knew Egypt well, and in 1964 reopened and ran the embassy in Cairo until Jacques Roux arrived as ambassador, whereupon the two of them divided responsibilities. His instructions were not to sacrifice Israel to the Arabs, but neither to sacrifice the Arabs to Israel. He made local friends and appreciated Egypt for its own sake, but the Quai d'Orsay and the Elysée were concerned mainly with the country's role in the Middle East conflict. To his chagrin, this relatively benign tack changed in the crisis of 1967, prompting him to the wry comment that de Gaulle had earned "the enthusiastic applause of the Arabs, the Soviets and all pro-Palestinians in France and elsewhere." De Gaulle's speech about the Jews as a self-assured and domineering people, Froment-Meurice continues, caused him pain (*"me fit mal"*).

In April 1979 he visited Israel, and its vulnerability in a universe of violence and terror struck him. This was all the more distressing because of the coldness with which his government was responding to the peace treaty just signed between Egypt and Israel. In a spirit of critical self-examination and confession completely alien to everything the Quai d'Orsay stood for, he wondered whether "France had suddenly become blind and deaf, or whether it was led to sacrifice peace by the idea it had of its interests, or whether pride and disappointment at not being associated with diplomatic activity took priority over sober judgment." Here, then, was a diplomat almost uniquely willing to do justice to Arabs and Israelis alike.

One other diplomat out of the ordinary was Alain Pierret, ambassador in Israel from 1986 to 1991. At a previous posting in Moscow, he had been occupied with the Helsinki Treaty, and in particular doing what he could on behalf of the refuseniks, those Jews wishing to emigrate to Israel but persecuted for it. During his six years as ambassador, he records in his memoirs, the Quai d'Orsay expected him to pressure the Israeli government to agree to an international conference, on the grounds that France could not accept exclusion from the peace process. He speaks of the "Israelophobia prevalent in some Parisian circles." When Arafat was officially invited to Paris in 1989, Pierret wrote to his colleague Patrick Leclercq, about to take over as head of the Afrique-Levant department: "It is one thing to have a perfectly understandable and justified pro-Arab policy, but something else to practice a kind of rampant anti-Zionism which forbids us from playing the role we legitimately claim. The Israelis are not deceived. And the mistake of receiving Arafat on May 2 has not helped." Later, when an act of PLO terror on the main road to Jerusalem killed sixteen people, the Quai d'Orsay put out a statement not condemning but merely "deplor[ing] the incident." France, Pierret concludes from his experience, was ceaselessly trying not to displease Palestinians without in fact satisfying them. For their part, "the Israelis will not have overlooked the pusillanimity we display towards them." In an article in *Libération* on October 26, 2000, he came to the still more lapidary judgment that France had chosen to join the Palestinian camp, and it would be only honest to admit it: "away with the hypocrisy and lies which for far too long have guided our Near East policy."

SIXTEEN

Pillars of Unwisdom

B<small>Y SUPPORTING</small> Saddam Hussein and Yasser Arafat, France hoped to lever itself into the position of mastery in the Middle East that has been a goal for such a long time. As a superpower, the United States now had responsibility for keeping the peace in the region, a difficult task with many facets. French policy therefore necessitated opposing the United States and Israel, but since both these states were nominally friendly, all sorts of pretexts and prevaricating formulæ had to be devised in the pretense that France was really cooperative, and promoting peace out of pure disinterest. France had little choice except to participate in the Gulf War of 1991. Disastrously, Arafat threw his lot in with Saddam Hussein, and Palestinians danced in the streets with joy as Scud missiles hit Israel. On as many as nine occasions, French emissaries, including the Prime Minister Michel Rocard and the Arabists Claude Cheysson and Roland Dumas, had meetings with Arafat. For France, the discomfiture of both their preferred point-men was an embarrassment, momentarily. The Oslo peace process then unfolded without any French input.

As President from 1995 onwards, Jacques Chirac set about with determination to correct what he saw as this set-back. In 1996, he visited the Middle East no less than five times. That April, in a speech in Cairo, he claimed that France intended to follow its traditional policies in the Middle East with renewed vigor. Chirac had advised Arafat to appeal to him in any emergency, and Arafat liked to quip that he could call on "Dr. Chirac." All that year, PLO and Hizbollah terror had been escalating with the introduction of suicide bombing. Israeli responses designed to frustrate such campaigns also undermined the position and legitimacy of Arafat, the instigator. Flying in to Paris, Arafat pleaded for France to come to his rescue.

Wasting no time, Chirac duly obliged, arranging a stop-over in Israel that October. Accompanying him was Leila Shahid, the PLO representative in Paris. Chirac and his party were staying in the King David Hotel in Jerusalem. In his book, *Les Secrets d'un ambassadeur*, Avi Pazner, the Israeli ambassador in Paris, recounts how Chirac's spokeswoman had been briefing journalists to be sure to cover Chirac's forthcoming visit to the Old City. Sure enough, he staged an incident. On his walk he refused the protection of uniformed Israeli police, he objected to the subsequent presence of plainclothesmen, and he switched route unexpectedly to find his way into the crowded Arab market. As Israeli security guards closed around to protect him, he shouted at them to stop, and threatened to fly back to Paris. His destination was Saint Anne's, a church in that Crusader style which in the eyes of so many generations of French officials is the rightful basis of French claims in the Middle East, and there Chirac once again played to the gallery, refusing to enter until Israeli police left. He then told the Arabs waiting in the church that he supported their political rights. That evening, he hosted a reception for Palestinians at the consulate-general. At a corresponding reception in the embassy in Tel Aviv, French citizens were invited but not a single Israeli.

Next day, with Leila Shahid more than ever welcome in his entourage, he flew by helicopter to Ramallah on the West Bank. He was the first world leader to address the Palestinian Legislative Council. Before an audience containing an ecstatic Arafat and other P L O leaders, he declared that Palestinian democracy might serve as an example to all Arab states (though how this might be so, and whether there was any Palestinian democracy, he did not pause to ask). Afterwards Arafat presented him with a decoration, the Star of Palestine. Moving on to Amman in Jordan, he touched on his other favorite topic, denouncing Western sanctions on Saddam Hussein.

This idiosyncratic odyssey triggered applause in the Arab world, and amazement elsewhere. It was not without consequences, however. Thanks to French pressure, the European Union took it upon itself to become Arafat's paymaster, to the tune of hundreds of millions of dollars, much of which either sponsored anti-Israel terror or was siphoned off into secret accounts abroad in Arafat's name. French pressure also induced the European Union to formalize at a summit in Barcelona the so-called Euro-Mediterranean Partnership between the EU and twelve southern Mediterranean countries. In the manner characteristic of the EU, this initiative is bogged down in bureaucracy, but in origin it is a mutation—and enhancement—of the concept of France as *"une puissance musulmane."* Indeed, Bat Ye'or, the authoritative analyst of this topic, considers that at Barcelona the EU was treating with "an imaginary Arab world." What the Barcelona Declaration actually produced was "a crescendo of Arab anti-Zionism and anti-American violence." This and similar initiatives, Bat Ye'or argues, have been so many steps in the evolution of Eurabia, the title of her book, as well as her coinage for a continent and its culture in the process of surrendering voluntarily to Arab supremacy.

The United Nations was the arena in which France chose to sponsor Saddam Hussein. There were reasons. During the 1980s, France had sold Iraq arms costing some 25 billion dollars, a sizable proportion of which remained to be paid. Sanctions alone prevented French oil companies from developing huge concessions in Iraqi oil fields. As France in its own estimation had gained from coming to the aid of Arafat, so now aid to Saddam Hussein would enable it to satisfy the long desired ambition of amounting to a counterweight to the United States and Britain, otherwise *les anglo-saxons*, that dreaded hybrid dating from Vichy of much French intellectual discourse. France has a veto in the Security Council and could also count in the UN on the support of Germany and Russia—the last time these three countries had been in an axis together was 1940 and to sizable parts of their populations the prospect of defying American hegemony (another term of fantasy in intellectual discourse) was now exhilarating. And more obscurely but vitally, pro-Arab sentiment provided cover for the self-enrichment of the happy few.

In the run-up to the second Gulf crisis of 2003, Chirac and his foreign minister Dominique de Villepin did their utmost to protect Saddam Hussein from both the consequences of his brutality to his own people and the folly of his bluster towards the rest of the world. Within the Elysée, a special policy group was formed and an emissary, Pierre Delval, dispatched to sound out "the possibility of change without war." Delval was to spend two weeks in every four on this political mission in Baghdad. Chirac sought to extend the remit of the UN weapons inspectors indefinitely, and so head off any military campaign. Having supported UN Resolution 1441 stating that Saddam's failure to co-operate entailed "serious consequences," Chirac then declared that France would oppose a second resolution designed to put the previous one into effect, "whatever the circumstances." To judge by his conduct, Saddam believed that France was indeed taking an initiative that would save him. In reality, Chirac's threat gave free rein to the United States and its coalition to act on their own, thus sealing Saddam's downfall. Military operations opened a few days later, and it was soon obvious that France had succeeded only in prejudicing its position in a future Iraq, indeed cutting itself out. Asked whether he wanted the Americans or Saddam to win, an embittered Villepin could not give an answer. *Les Cent Semaines* is a book about Villepin's time as foreign minister, and in it is a description of a meeting at the Quai d'Orsay at which an official offers the opinion that the military campaign against Saddam Hussein will be short. "That is not desirable. France would appear ridiculous," was Villepin's retort.

Soon after the liberation of Iraq, the press started to reveal how Saddam Hussein had defeated the UN sanctions by means of a gigantic scam, reaching deep into the UN and negating whatever moral authority it liked to claim. The UN had permitted him to sell Iraqi oil on condition that the money was used for humanitarian purposes. A large number of companies and individuals were authorized to participate in this oil-for-food program, and it turned out that Saddam Hussein had suborned or bribed many of them. These assorted profiteers skimmed off money for themselves and handed kickbacks to Saddam Hussein and his fellows in the order of billions of dollars, a scale outdoing the corruption even of the Mitterrand era.

People of numerous nationalities participated in this racketeering and among them were eleven Frenchmen, including Charles Pasqua, once Minister of the Interior; his diplomatic advisor Bernard Guillet; Gilles Munier, secretary general of the Franco-Iraqi Friendship Society; and two "*ambassadeurs de France*," Jean-Bernard Mérimée and Serge Boidevaix. Investigation by an examining magistrate confirmed that the former of these two ambassadors had received $165,000 and the latter about $200,000. Both were also accused of abusing their position for the sake of personal gain (*"trafic d'influence"*). Mérimée admitted to the examining magistrate that he had not declared this money for tax purposes. It is a particular embarrassment that these diplomats had been involved in setting up the oil-for-food program in the first place.

Mérimée, a descendant of the novelist's brother, had been a close collaborator of Giscard's and in 1987 he was appointed ambassador in Morocco. Apparently on the orders of the late King Hassan II, and seemingly in return for favors done in unblocking a large sum in a Moroccan bank, he was presented with a property at Ourzazate, described by a critical French publication as one of several "magnificent villas" built for special but unspecified purposes. From 1991 to 1995, he served as ambassador and France's permanent representative at the UN. It fell to him to negotiate an important Security Council resolution with Tarik Aziz, then Saddam Hussein's foreign minister, and the weekly magazine *L'Express* accused him in an article on October 20, 2005 of "intense lobbying in favor of Saddam Hussein's Iraq."

Boidevaix had once been the right-hand man of the Arabist Jobert. As diplomatic advisor to Chirac in 1974 he had been instrumental in selling the Osirak nuclear reactor to Iraq. He arranged three of the meetings Chirac had with Saddam Hussein. In 1980 he became head of

the North African and Middle East department and twelve
years later reached the peak of his career as secretary
general of the Quai d'Orsay. In retirement, he served
from 2002 onwards as President of the Franco-Arab
Chamber of Commerce. Boidevaix's lawyer claimed that
his client had kept the Quai d'Orsay fully in the picture,
"in order to be sure that his activities did not injure
French policy." Stifling the scandal as best it could, the
Quai d'Orsay set up an internal "ethical committee."

Like other Presidents before him, Chirac was in all
probability neither a racist nor an anti-Semite. As anti-
Jewish attacks began to mount as from the beginning of
the new millennium, he liked to insist that there was no
anti-Semitism in France. In the face of the accumulating
evidence, however, he changed course, condemning the
French role in deporting Jews to their death during the
war, and even apologizing for it, and he has made robust
statements in defense of French Jews under attack today.
Yet through his unconditional support for Arafat and
the PLO he willingly became the accomplice of a man
and an organization responsible for the death of thousands of Jews, and the injuring of a great many more. Nor
was this his only anti-Jewish measure. Lebanese Hizbollah, an Iranian proxy, has also killed many Jews, and
Chirac went out of his way to welcome its leader, Sheikh
Hassan Nasrallah, at a Francophone summit. Alone among
Western heads of state, Chirac attended the funeral of
Hafiz al-Assad, the Syrian dictator implacably opposed
to peace with Israel except on his own absolute terms.

The second intifada broke out in September 2000.

The following month, Arafat and Israeli Prime Minister Ehud Barak met in Paris for a tense summit brokered by Madeleine Albright. Moments before the agreement to a cease-fire was about to materialize, Chirac telephoned Arafat with the advice not to sign but to hold out for more concessions. So there was no agreement. Barak's chief of staff said that Chirac's intervention "turned this thing on its head" though a spokesman for Chirac countered that he had merely pleaded for "appeasement."

The intifada was still raging in the summer of 2004, and suicide bombers claiming their victims regularly, when French foreign Minister Michel Barnier visited Ramallah to announce, "I have come to deliver the cordial greetings of the president of the French Republic in these difficult times." That October, Arafat fell ill. Chirac sent a French government plane to fly him to Paris, to be treated in a military hospital. Amid maximum publicity, Chirac visited Arafat's bedside. The very next day, he gave another vivid illustration of his mind-set, when he flew to congratulate the new ruler of the United Arab Emirates rather than keep to a scheduled meeting with the interim Iraqi prime minister of the post-Saddam Hussein regime, and so avoid anything that might have looked like a pro-American gesture. When Arafat then died, Chirac arranged ceremonies suitable for a head of state, with a guard of honor of French soldiers to carry the coffin to the aircraft transporting it back to Ramallah. At this event, his eyes watering, he declared, "With him disappears a man of courage and conviction. . . . I came to bow before President Yasser Arafat and pay him final homage." In sober fact, with him disappeared a man with half a century of death-dealing violence and corruption behind him, a man above all who had failed his own people. With him also disappeared the man who had so skilfully played on the self-importance of French leaders, luring them on to act as though they could be arbiters of the Middle East. The expectations arising from befriending Arafat were a repeat of the expectations placed in Haj Amin and Khomeini, and so dominant is the in-built illusion that no amount of experience dispels it.

CONCLUSION

FRANCE TODAY does not have the resources or the influence either to supplant the United States or to enlist the Arab world, to create a state of Palestine or to dismantle Israel. The intimacy of its relationship with the tyrannies of Saddam Hussein's Iraq and Arafat's Palestine Authority finally depleted its political and—graver still—its moral authority. In the Middle East, France has forfeited whatever leverage it might once have enjoyed, and even deserved to enjoy, if its claim to be protector of the Holy Land is entertained.

France nevertheless continues to behave in defiance of reality, on the assumption that it has only to pursue its political agenda regardless. One decision after another betrays an attitude impervious to the unfolding of events. To be sure, much of what France now undertakes amounts to mere pin-pricks in the international spectrum, but still of nuisance value to the parties at the receiving end, while precipitously degrading to France itself. The catalogue is so comprehensive, yet so formalized, that its practitioners seem representatives of a special culture all their own, quite unconscious of the figures they cut, as though a spectral procession of the likes of Ratti-Menton and de Caix, Massignon and Neuville, is holding their successors in thrall.

Much time will have to pass in order to repair the breach France so deliberately sought with the United States by protecting Saddam Hussein and Arafat. France's animus against Jewish self-determination has been settled for such a long period that it has hardened into place, and nothing seems likely to cause any revision of this ingrained opposition to Israel in matters petty or significant. At the end of the fighting in former Yugoslavia, for instance, Israel offered asylum to one hundred Bosnian Muslims, but the Quai d'Orsay refused to participate in their transportation for fear of "promoting Israeli propaganda." In 1996, Hizbollah launched rocket attacks on northern Israel. Israel's subsequent measures of self-defense, Prime Minister Alain Juppé said, were "inadmissable." The Quai d'Orsay then condemned Israeli containment of Hizbollah in southern Lebanon, and dragged out the attempt to block the Hizbollah television station Al-Manar from spreading its hatred of Jews via a Paris-based satellite (although finally this was forbidden). Sophie Pommier, the official responsible in the ministry for following Israeli-Palestinian negotiations, revealed her emotional involvement by plastering the walls of her office with portraits of Arafat; French consulates are forbidden from recognizing weddings by West Bank rabbis; Stanislas de Laboulaye, consul general in Jerusalem cultivating links to both Hamas and the PLO, described himself as "French ambassador to

Palestine." Although Palestinians burnt out one site holy to Jews, the Quai d'Orsay criticized the protective annexation of Rachel's Tomb, another Jewish holy site, near Bethlehem. Muslims alone are permitted to enter Mecca, but the Quai d'Orsay and other French ministries have opened a consulate there, and issued a document advising about travel arrangements, and including the sentence, "The pilgrimage to Mecca is a voyage every Muslim hopes for." Such official piety in a Christian context is unthinkable.

More: The Quai d'Orsay sent Gilbert Béréziat, president of Paris VI university, to Al-Najah university in Nablus in the knowledge that he had voted against his campus's agreement to cooperate with Israeli universities; Jacques Huntziger, ambassador in Tel Aviv, slammed his fist on the table and left the room when the parents of three Israeli soldiers captured by Hizbollah asked him to intervene on their behalf after a visit by Chirac to Lebanon; Gérard Araud, the current ambassador in Tel Aviv, declared in December 2004 that "Israelis suffer from a neurosis, a veritable mental disorder which makes them anti-French." During the first Gulf War, Daniel Bernard had been the spokesman for the Quai d'Orsay, and perceived by the press as pro-Arab. Promoted ambassador to London, at a dinner party he openly called Israel "a shitty little country." During the second intifada, France refused to sell anti-riot material to Israel.

And still more: François Bujon de l'Estang, French ambassador in Washington, cancelled a meeting with American Jewish and Christian groups because he did not want to be questioned about anti-Semitism in France. Writing in *Le Nouvel Observateur*, Foreign Minister Védrine maintained that blaming the collapse of the Camp David negotiations on Arafat was Israeli "propaganda." Never elected to any position, Prime Minister Dominique de Villepin owes his advancement to the whims of Chirac. In 2001, at a time when he was Chirac's secretary general at the Elysée, de Villepin is said to have forecast to a prominent journalist the disappearance of Israel on the grounds that it was merely "a parenthesis in history." France refuses to take action against the Comité de Bienfaisance et de Secours aux Palestiniens (CBSP) although this organization funnels money to Hamas terrorism, and is also pressing the EU not to place restrictions on financial aid that must end in the hands of Hamas. Leaders of Hamas like to insist that they will destroy Israel, yet when they won the Palestinian Legislative elections in 2005 and formed a government, the Quai d'Orsay broke ranks with other Western foreign ministries and opened a back-channel with a view to establishing which of Hamas's demands could be met.

When President Ahmadinejad of Iran declared that Israel had to be wiped off the map, Chirac's response to this Hitlerite promise of genocide was merely that Iran now risked being "banned from the international community." In July 2006, Hizbollah once again crossed the international border to kill and abduct Israelis. Chirac lost no time condemning Israeli measures of self-defense to this open act of war as "totally disproportionate," and even evidence of "a sort of will to destroy Lebanon."

Conclusion

Iran makes no secrfet of the fact that it arms, finances, and trains Hizbollah, thus becoming responsible for the aggressions of its proxy. In another example of outright defiance of reality, Philippe Douste-Blazy, the French foreign minister, saw fit to pronounce that Iran is "a stabilizing influence" in the region.Speaking for the Socialists and therefore open to the charge of playing party politics, François Hollande nevertheless put his finger on what is amiss when he suggested that the presidency should cede foreign policy to the National Assembly because of "the tendency that goes back a long way, and is called France's Arab policy, and it is not acceptable for an administration to have an ideology."

The natural fulfilment of the historic contempt for Israel as a mainstay of Jewish identity is to call into question the position of Jews in French society. For an almost equal period of time, Arabs have been accustomed to the cajolery of the French state, and the expected privilege that goes with it. These two long-drawn but incompatible approaches have finally come to a head, and collided. Commitment to the Palestinians in their conflict with Israel incites the growing underclass of Arabs first to resent Jews, and then to force into the public arena the contradiction whereby the French state claims to be protecting Jews at home while doing what it can to oppose Jews in Israel. Confusion that might have been contained at its origins in the Middle East is therefore exploding in the everyday violence experienced in French cities and towns. More than just social disruption between different communities, here is also a seed-bed for Islamist jihad.

Conclusion

In the course of 2004, Israeli Prime Minister Ariel Sharon urged French Jews to move out of harm's way by emigrating to Israel. France is host, he said, to "the wildest anti-Semitism." As though to substantiate this point, Chirac responded that Sharon would not be welcome in France. "Hitler has a son—Sharon" was daubed on Paris walls in the deteriorating climate of opinion; in a protective measure reminiscent of the 1930s, Grand Rabbi Sitruk advised observant Jews not to wear a skullcap in the open street. Whether out of alarm or perhaps penitence for past misconceptions that he had done much to perpetuate, Chirac felt obliged to emphasize even more strongly that French Jews do indeed face general anti-Semitism on the part of the country's Arabs and other Muslims; and that in words of his, spoken after the burning of a Jewish school in a Paris suburb, "An attack against a French Jew is an attack against France."

This realization is belated. The French state's hostility to Jewish self-determination coincides with Arab and Muslim resentment and fuels corresponding violence. The sustained attempt to fit Arabs and Jews into a grand design on French terms has set the two communities against one another, while also advancing to crisis point the relationship of both to the French state. France is acquiring an internal reality as "une puissance musulmane" on lines quite different from anything envisaged by those who have fostered this intellectual illusion, and it is proving highly dangerous to the interests of everyone concerned.

ACKNOWLEDGMENTS

THANKS ARE DUE to French friends who showed me the way through the archives of the Quai d'Orsay, and encouraged the writing of this book. They do not wish to be named. M.A.E. is the abbreviation for Ministère des Affaires Etrangères, and Afrique-Levant is generally the department within it. In the text I have given references to such documents as seemed to require them, bearing in mind that the reader's patience is unnecessarily taxed by repetition of references, especially from the same series of volumes. The translations are my own.

Thanks are also due to *Commentary* magazine, in whose issue dated May 2005 there appeared the essay which gave rise to this revised and extended version. Publishing that essay in *Commentaire*, the magazine he edits in Paris, Jean-Claude Casanova provided material concerning Claudel and also the Cambon brothers which I have incorporated. Roger Kimball has been the kind of encouraging publisher every writer hopes for.

A very special salute goes to Clarissa, my wife, for the exemplary way she tolerated and even encouraged the long paper-chase.

BIBLIOGRAPHY

THE FOLLOWING BIBLIOGRAPHY aims to list only the more important books I have relied on or to which I refer.

CHAPTER ONE: THE HARVEST.

Yves Charles Zarka, Sylvie Taussig, Cynthia Fleury, eds. *L'Islam en France.*

CHAPTER TWO: THE QUAI D'ORSAY.

Margaret Macmillan. *The Peacemakers: The Paris Conference of 1919.*
Gabriel Hanotaux. *Mon Temps.*
H. B. Haynes. *The French Foreign Office and the Origins of the First World War 1989–1914.*

CHAPTER THREE: JEWS IN THE VIEW OF THE QUAI D'ORSAY.

Jonathan Frankel. *The Damascus Affair.*
M.A.E./dossiers généraux du Personnel/Concours/Vol. 8 bis.
M.A.E./Personnel 2ᵉ série/Paul Blanc/Vol. 185.
J.-B. Barbier. *Un Frac de Nessus.*
Paul Cambon. *Correspondance, 1870–1924.*
Michel Drouin, ed. *L'Affaire Dreyfus de A à Z.*
Maurice Paléologue. *Journal de l'Affaire Dreyfus.*
Maurice Bompard. *Mon Ambassade en Russie.*
Maurice Paléologue. *La Russie des Tsars pendant la Grande Guerre.*
Maurice Paléologue. *Les Précurseurs de Lénine.*

CHAPTER FOUR: THE CATHOLIC FACTOR.

Pierre Guillen. *L'Expansion 1881–1898.*
Jacques Thobie. *La France et l'Est méditerranéen depuis 1850.*
Moussa Abou Ramadan. *Les Accords de Mytilène de 1901 et l'agrément*

Bibliography

de Constantinople de 1913 in *De Bonaparte à Balfour* (Dominique Trimbur and Ran Aaronsohn, eds.)

Gabriel Hanotaux. *Mon Temps* IV.

Maurice Pernot. *Rapport sur Voyage d'Etude à Constantinople, en Egypte et en Turquie d'Asie. Janvier-août 1912.*

CHAPTER FIVE: ZIONISM VERSUS FRENCH DESIGNS.

Louis Bertrand. *Le Mirage oriental.*

Comte de Saint-Aulaire. *Confession d'un vieux diplomate.*

Edy Kaufman. *The French Pro-Zionist Declarations of 1917–1918. Middle Eastern Studies* 15 (1979), 374–407.

CHAPTER SIX: BETWEEN THE WARS.

Christopher M. Andrew and A. S. Kanya-Forstner. *France Overseas.*

Christopher M. Andrew and A. S. Kanya-Forstner. *La France à la recherche de la Syrie intégrale 1914–1920.*

Peter A. Shambrook. *French Imperialism in Syria 1927–1936.*

Michel Abitbol. *Les Deux Terres promises.*

Marie-Renée Mouton. *La Société des Nations et les intérêts de la France (1920–1924).*

Henri Laurens. *Le Royaume impossible.*

André Gillois. *Histoire secrète des Français à Londres de 1940 à 1944.*

CHAPTER SEVEN: WRITERS TAKE SIDES.

Jean-Luc Barré, Philippe Berthelot. *L'Eminence grise 1866–1934.*

Jean-François Fogel. *Morand-Express.*

Ralph Schor. *L'Antisémitisme en France pendant les années trente.*

Christopher Flood. *Penseé politique et imagination historique dans l'œuvre de Paul Claudel.*

Cahiers Paul Claudel 7. *La Figure d'Israël.*

Chapter Eight. *The Rescue of the Mufti of Jerusalem.*

Max Egremont. *Under Two Flags. The Life of Major-General Sir Edward Spears.*

Henri Laurens. *Le Mufti et la France de la IV République.*

CHAPTER EIGHT: THE MYSTIQUE OF LOUIS MASSIGNON.

Elie Kedourie. "Politics and the Academy" in *Commentary*, August 1992.

Robert Irwin. *The Lust for Knowing.*

Christian Destremau and Jean Moncelon. *Louis Massignon.*

Bibliography

Amira El-Zein. "L'Autre dans la spiritualité massignonienne" in *Louis Massignon au cœur de notre temps*, ed. Jacques Keryell.

Jacques Keryell. "Louis Massignon et la Syrie," op. cit.

Jacques Keryell, ed. *Louis Massignon et ses contemporains.*

"Louis Massignon et la Palestine." hhtp:jm.saliege.com/palestine.htm.

Daniel Massignon, ed. *Louis Massignon et le dialogue des cultures.*

André Chouraqui. *La Reconnaissance. Le Saint-Siège, les Juifs et Israël.*

Michel Malicet, ed. *Paul Claudel Louis Massignon (1908–1914). Correspondance établie et annotée.*

CHAPTER TEN: "A PERNICIOUS EXAMPLE AND A GREAT PERIL."

Mélanges en l'honneur de Jean-Baptiste Duroselle, Enjeux et Puissances.

Christian Pineau. *Mémoires.*

Jean Chauvel. *Commentaire. D'Alger à Berne 1944–1952.*

Georges Dethan. *Le Quai d'Orsay de 1945 à 1981* in *Collection de l'Ecole Française de Rome* 54/3.

Jacques Dumaine. *Quai d'Orsay 1945–1951.*

Tsilla Hershco. *Entre Paris et Jérusalem* (doctorate originally in Hebrew).

Vincent Auriol. *Journal du septennat.*

CHAPTER ELEVEN: TAKING ADVANTAGE.

Sylvia K. Crosbie. *A Tacit Alliance: France and Israel from Suez to the Six Day War.*

Abel Thomas. *Comment Israël fut sauvé.*

Christian Pineau. *1956 Suez.*

J.-R. Tournoux. *Secrets d'Etat.*

Bernard Destremau. *Quai d'Orsay: Derrière la façade.*

Michel Bar-Zohar. *Suez, Ultra secret.*

Robert Paul Grant. *Les Querelles Franco-Américaines* (doctorate, Institut d'Etudes Politiques de Paris).

Maurice Couve de Murville. *La France dans le monde.*

Samir Kassir and Farouk Mardam-Bey. *Itinéraires de Paris à Jérusalem.*

S. Cohen. *Les Gaullistes et l'Etat d'Israël* (doctorate, Ecole pratique des Hautes Etudes). Samy Cohen. *De Gaulle, les gaullistes et Israël.*

Claude Clément. *Israël et la Vᵉ République.*

Zach Levey. *Israel and the Western Powers.*

Michael Bar-Zohar. *Embassies in Crisis: Diplomats and Demagogues Behind the Six-Day War.*

Howard M. Sachar. *Israel and Europe.*

Bibliography

Raymond Aron. *De Gaulle and the Jews.*
P. Wajsman and R.-F. Teissèdre. *Nos Politiciens face au conflit Israélo-Arabe.*
Charles de Gaulle. *Mémoires.*
Jack Gee. *Le Mirage.*

CHAPTER TWELVE: MEN AND MATTERS.

Claude Clément, *op. cit.*
Philippe de Saint-Robert. *Les Septennats interrompus.*
Howard M. Sachar, *op. cit.*
Thierno Diallo. *La politique étrangère de Georges Pompidou.*
Maurice Szafran. *Les Juifs dans la politique française de 1945 à nos jours.*
Hervé Alphand. *L'Etonnement d'être: Journal 1939–1973.*
Jean-Louis Remilleux. *Ni Dieu ni diable.*
Michel Jobert. *Les Illusions immobiles.*

CHAPTER THIRTEEN: INTERESTS AND HEARTS.

Hervé Alphand, *op. cit.*
Nicolas Beau. *Paris, capitale arabe.*
Claude Kutschera ed. *Le Livre noir de Saddam Hussein*
Howard M. Sachar, *op. cit.*

CHAPTER FOURTEEN: THE PURSUIT OF THE AYATOLLAH.

Mohammad Reza Pahlavi. *Answer to History.*
Christian Delannoy and Jean-Pierre Pichard. *Khomeini: La Révolution trahie.*
Mir Ali Asghar Montazem. *The Life and Times of Ayatollah Khomeini.*
Amir Taheri. *The Spirit of Allah.*
Fereydoun Hoveyda. *The Fall of the Shah.*
Jimmy Carter. *Keeping Faith.*
Abol Hasan Bani Sadr. *My Turn to Speak.*
Pierre Péan. *La Menace.*

CHAPTER FIFTEEN: INS AND SOME OUTS.

Jean Bourdeillette. *Pour Israël.*
Henri Froment-Meurice. *Vu du Quai.*
Alain Pierret. *Ambassadeur en Israël.*

CHAPTER SIXTEEN: PILLARS OF UNWISDOM.

Avi Pazner. *Les Secrets d'un ambassadeur.*
Bat Ye'or. *Eurabia.*

INDEX

Index

Assad, Hafiz al-, 144
Attali, Jacques: *Verbatim*, 106
Aube, L' (journal), 73
Auden, W. H., 55
Auriol, Vincent, 81
Austria: Hitler invades (1938), 47
Ayatollah, the, *see* Khomeini, Ayatollah Ruhollah
Aziz, Tariq, 120, 143
Azoury, Najib: *Le Réveil de la Nation arabe*, 31

Baath Party: in Iraq, 117
Bakhtiar, Shapour, 129
Balfour, Arthur James, 30, 35–6; Declaration on Jewish national home, 34, 113
Bani Sadr, Abol Hasan, 127
Bar-Zohar, Michael, 96
Barak, Ehud, 144–5
Barbier, Jean-Baptiste: *Un Frac de Nessus*, 21–2
Barcelona Declaration, 140
Barnier, Michel, 132, 135
Barre, Raymond, 114, 119
Baudoin, Paul, 48
Baudrillart, Cardinal Alfred-Henri-Marie, 57
Baverez, Nicolas, 4
Beau, Nicolas: *Paris, Capitale Arabe*, 115
Beaudin, Jean-Baptiste, 19
Begin, Menachem, 79
Beirut: Lebanese civil aircraft blown up by Israelis, 97; Arafat rescued from, 108
Ben-Gurion, David, 78, 90, 92, 94, 133
Ben-Natan, Asher, 101

Benchallali, Chelali, 9
Benda, Julien: *La Trahison des clercs*, 68
Béréziat, Gilbert, 149
Bernard, Daniel, 149
Bernard, Gaston, 47
Berthelot, Hélène, 50
Berthelot, Philippe, 31, 44–5, 50–1, 70
Bertrand, Louis: *Le Mirage Oriental*, 29
Bidault, Georges, 61, 76
Bihourd, Georges, 22
Binaud, Jean, 86
Binoche, Jean, 85
Black September (group), 103
Blanc, Paul, 21
Blum, Léon, 30
Bohlen, Charles, 96–7
Boidevaix, Serge, 142–4
Bompard, Maurice, 24
Boumedienne, Adel, 13
Bourdeillette, Jean: *Pour Israël*, 133
Bourgès-Manoury, Maurice, 90, 91
Brezhnev, Leonid, 111
Briand, Aristide, 39, 42
Britain: and founding of Jewish national home, 34; granted mandate in Palestine, 37, 41, 78; and Muslim discontent with Jews in Jerusalem, 38; France accuses of complicity with Jews in Palestine, 39; ban on arms sales to Middle East belligerents, 89; in Suez crisis (1956), 91
Buber, Martin, 73

Index

Index

Index

Index

A Note on the Type

B ETRAYAL has been set in Bodoni Old Face, a type derived from the many faces cut by the Italian printer Giambattista Bodoni (1740–1813). The son of a Piedmontese printer, Bodoni began his career as a compositor at the Vatican's Press of Propagation of the Faith. In 1768, he was named head of the ducal printing house in Parma, where he pursued his most important work as printer and typographer. Innovative in both design and technique, Bodoni's books were admired for their meticulous prersswork, opulent production, and generous formats— though his reputation as a printer of scholarly works was diminished by poor proofreading. While Bodoni's early work was executed under the influence of the Fourniers, the family of French typefounders and printers, it was the work of the English printer John Baskerville that would most profoundly color his later output as a punchcutter and designer of books. The types Bodoni cut at the Stamperia Reale, considered the first "modern" faces, are widely admired for the pronounced contract between thick and thin strokes, for their fine serifs, and for their openness and delicacy.

DESIGN AND COMPOSITION BY CARL W. SCARBROUGH